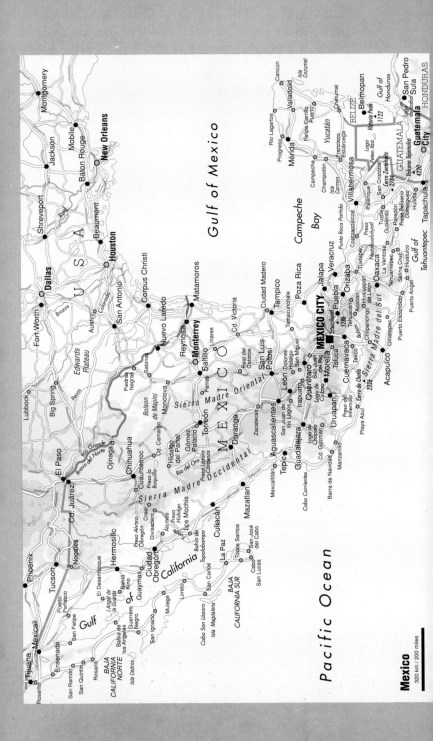

Mexico
320 km / 200 miles

Welcome!

A vast accretion of tiny rural villages which is rapidly becoming the largest metropolis in the world, Mexico City is a rich and complex city that surprises and inspires. In these pages Insight's correspondent in Mexico City helps makes sense of its chaos while celebrating its flamboyant style.

Margaret King has lived in Mexico City for over 25 years, teaching, translating and studying. She still delights in the great charm of the city, where the rustic sound of a crowing rooster can be heard outside a window off sophisticated Paseo de la Reforma Avenue, where sleep is interrupted by the sound of guitars rather than dogs barking and where Indians are a living presence.

The carefully crafted tours she has devised for this book begin with the downtown area, where brightly colored pyramids once dominated the landscape, continue with the Zona Rosa, with its concentration of international restaurants, and then move to the neighborhoods of San Angel and Coyoacán, which retain the flavor of a bygone age. She has also devised a range of day trips outside the city – to Teotihuacán, whose main pyramid rivals that of Cheops in Egypt in size and majesty; to Taxco, a hillside town famous for silver; and to Cuernavaca. Her suggestions are carefully paced and include stops for refreshment. They include the kind of tips that only someone intimately acquainted with a destination can share.

You probably won't end up staying on, like our correspondent did, but your visit will certainly be memorable and is unlikely to be your last.

Pages 8/9:
Rivera mural on the
Teatro Insurgentes

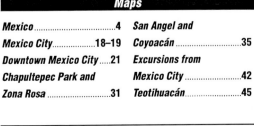

HISTORY & CULTURE

Situated on a plateau in the central highlands 2,286m (7,500ft) above sea level, the valley in which Mexico City is located has been inhabited since at least 10,000BC and was once a sweeping, forested green landscape with shining lakes, abundant game and fish, and large flocks of birds. Originally nomadic hunters, its people eventually settled in small villages at different points on the shores, taking advantage of the rich alluvial soils and benign climate for agriculture and developing increasingly complex cultures over the millennia. The earliest surviving ceremonial center is the Cuicuilco round pyramid complex in the south of the city, dating from 600BC.

Arrival of Aztecs

The Aztecs were latecomers to the valley and by the time of their arrival in the 12th century the nearby metropolis of Teotihuacán with its monumental pyramids had been abandoned for hundreds of years. The lands around the lakes were governed by several culturally distinct small empires – the names of some of the original towns are still familiar as components of the present-day metropolitan area: Cuautitlán, Atzapolzalco, Coyoacán, Xochimilco – whose different peoples regarded the less advanced, warlike Aztecs as barbarians.

The legendary wanderings of the Aztecs are said to have begun in AD1111 with their departure from the mythical city of Aztlán in the north, as recorded in the Boturini Codex. The Aztecs were searching for a sign from the gods that would indicate the spot where they should establish their city: an eagle perched on a cactus growing on a rock with a snake in its beak, a symbol used in modern Mexico's flag and official seals. Their ultimate decision to settle on the swampy island of Zoquitlán in Lake Texcoco probably came about through necessity rather than a divine sign. Despised by all after gravely offending the people of Culhuacán by killing their king's daughter in sacrifice to their god, the Aztecs were

Aztec pelota player

The national emblem

forced to take refuge in this inhospitable location, a veritable no-man's-land.

Despite the unpromising topography, the Aztecs applied their ingenuity and created land from the swamp. One account states that they sank tree trunks into the mud, creating a firmer foundation for building, while others take the view that it all began with the *chinampa* system, consisting of woven reed mats set afloat and covered with earth and then planted with crops. The resulting roots, which penetrated the shallow lake bottom, stabilized the structure and little by little the island grew. However it was done, by the time Cortés arrived, Tenochtitlán, as the new city was called, was one of the marvels of the world with a population of some 400,000 people and three wide causeways connecting the city to the shores.

A network of canals permitted the easy transport of people and goods. Tenochtitlán's palaces and pyramid-studded ceremonial center were painted in many colors and burnished to such a shining finish that the city was reputed to be made of silver. This impression may have been created at night, when the buildings shone in the silvery moonlight.

Frightening omens

The Aztec religion had a large pantheon of gods. Among the most important of these was Quetzalcoatl, represented as a bearded white man. According to legend, Quetzalcoatl had departed by sea, vowing to return. Eerily, the time of his prophesied return coincided with the arrival of the Spanish. Montezuma, the Aztec emperor, and his priests witnessed a series of omens around this time, which they took for signs of the imminent return of the god or the arrival of an invading force.

This may explain the cordial reception initially given to Cortés and his men. Hearing of the landing of the bearded white men, so like Quetzalcoatl's image, Montezuma despatched gifts, hoping to deter them from coming to Tenochtitlán and yet appeasing them, just in case this was the second coming of the deity.

Among the presents were pieces made of solid gold, which inflamed the Europeans' greed. The Spanish fully intended to con-

quer the Aztec city, having committed themselves by burning all but one of their ships. They had also obtained the services of 'La Malinche,' an Indian woman of noble descent, who played an indispensable role as interpreter and advisor.

One aspect of Montezuma's religion, that may have led to the downfall of the Aztec civilization, was human sacrifice, which was considered necessary to feed the gods. Without such sustenance, it was believed the world would come to an end, and with the expansion of their domain, the Aztecs intensified their sacrificial activity. In fact, the Aztecs waged what were called the 'Flower Wars' to obtain prisoners for sacrifice. This and the tribute exacted to sustain the empire created deep resentment throughout the land and other Indian peoples gladly allied themselves with the Spanish to defeat their common enemy.

Entry of Cortés

The Spanish were astounded at the sight of the fabled city of Tenochtitlàn, set in a lake against snow-capped volcanoes in the distance, and by their reception. Throngs of curious people came out to see these strange men on horseback, believed to be a type of centaur or perhaps to be mounted on deer (the horse being unknown on the continent). The initial encounter between Cortés and Montezuma was cordial and the Spanish were housed in one of the emperor's finest palaces. Relations deteriorated, however, with the inevitable religious conflicts. The emperor was taken prisoner and eventually died. The Indians, having realized that they were not dealing with deities, lost their fear of Spanish arms and horses and uprisings began. The final siege was laid in 1521, with the Spanish building a fleet of boats, having cut off the city's water supply. Outnumbered against the Spaniards who were superior in both weapons and tactics, as well as in coping with the ravages of smallpox and other diseases (to which the Indians had never been exposed), the Indians were defeated and the Aztec empire decimated. Bernal Díaz del Castillo describes the victors' entry into the capital. There were so many dead, he said, that they could not avoid treading on corpses.

By the 1560s, within 50 years of the Spaniards' arrival, the population of 30 million Indians had fallen to a tenth of that figure.

Hernán Cortés

The colonial city

The conquerors purposely built their city on the foundations of the razed Aztec buildings, using the stones to erect their churches and palaces, thus expressing their domination over the land and the beginning of a new rule. The first European buildings were veritable fortresses for protection in a still hostile territory.

Cortés withdrew to the town of Coyoacán after his victory, where he remained for two years. Thinking that their leader had kept the alleged Aztec treasure for himself, some conquistadors took to writing graffiti on the whitewashed walls of Cortés's house, some of it in an elegant, poetic style. Cortés was calm in answering these accusations, replying (according to Bernal Díaz de Castillo): 'A blank wall is a fool's writing paper.'

The Spanish crown sent the first viceroy to govern what was now New Spain in 1530. Missionaries from different orders arrived and the city became liberally dotted with convents and monasteries. Religion again dominated life in the city and the Catholic Church came to own a large portion of the colony's territory. The first university in the continent, the Royal Pontifical University of Mexico (today's National University of Mexico), was established in 1553. The Inquisition was established in 1571.

An aristocracy grew up based on titles granted by the king of Spain (often on account of the fabulous wealth of the title seekers). Their houses were adorned with coats of arms, some of which, still in place, can be seen in the downtown area today.

The surrounding lake, with its periodic floods, was a major problem. The flood of 1629 lasted for five years, destroying most of the buildings from the previous century; transportation in the streets was only possible by boat; Mass was held on rooftops.

By the 18th century, Mexico City truly lived up to its name as 'the City of Palaces', with clean, well-lit streets, magnificent churches, most with intricately worked gold altarpieces and other luxurious

The National Palace

adornments intended to transmit the idea of 'Heaven on earth.' The city, which had still not grown beyond Alameda Park, was a most pleasant place to live.

However, all positions of power were legally in the hands of peninsular Spaniards born in Spain, while those of pure Spanish descent born in Mexico, the *criollos,* were denied any opportunity to govern. Those of mixed Spanish-Indian or *mestizo* heritage were relegated to the lower rungs of society and Indians and black Africans and mulattos were at the very bottom. A rigid caste system operated for the different racial compositions of the population.

Independence from Spain

The *criollos'* chafing under the heavy hand of Spain came to a head in the person of Father Miguel Hidalgo whose *Grito* (call for independence) in 1810 triggered a brave but premature uprising. Mexico didn't gain her independence until 11 years later.

The early years of independence were beset with problems. One of the presidents, Santa Ana, a vain and ambitious man, led Mexico to a disastrous war with the United States in 1846–48, which led to massive loss of Mexican territory. US forces even captured Mexico City, where the boy cadets manning Chapultepec Castle fought to the last boy, earning them a place in history as the *Niños Héroes* (Boy Heroes).

Maximilian of Hapsburg

One of Mexico's greatest leaders, Benito Juárez, came to power in 1855. He broke up the extensive land and property holdings of the Church; ordered nuns and monks to abandon their cloisters and established the formal separation of Church and State in the constitution. Many churches were sacked and stripped of their fabulous ornamentation, much to the consternation of the conservatives, who backed Maximilian of Hapsburg's overthrow of Júarez in 1864. The city owes its grandest avenue to Maximilian, the Paseo de la Reforma, which, legend maintains, the Empress Carlotta wanted built so that she could watch her husband riding to the National Palace from her vantage point in Chapultepec Castle. Juárez recovered power and ordered the execution of the Austrian prince in 1867, as a firm statement that foreign powers should not meddle in Mexican affairs.

The Porfiriato, depicted by the muralist Siqueiros

The Porfiriato

The election of General Porfirio Díaz to the presidency in 1876, began a 35-year period called the *Porfiriato,* after the president-dictator. In an apparent attempt to create a Parisian-style atmosphere, the city gained buildings in a mélange of European styles, with French predominating. The nation's railroad was also built during this time. Though modernization was the byword, power and wealth were held by very few, with a number of *hacienda* ranches reaching the size of some European countries.

The assassination of Francisco Madero in 1910 set off the sparks of the Mexican Revolution, which continued until 1921, devastating the countryside but providing heroes of legend, including Pancho Villa and Emiliano Zapata, who are known the world over.

After the Revolution, Mexican values were rediscovered. In the 1920s the great Diego Rivera began covering the walls of public buildings with murals idealizing the pre-Hispanic past and portraying the Spanish as villains. He worked with a gun in his belt – 'to orient the critics,' who did not appreciate his subject matter.

He loved to shock. On a mural in the now demolished Prado Hotel (the mural was moved to the Alameda Museum behind the Alameda Park) he wrote: 'God does not exist.' The words caused such an uproar that they had to be expunged.

Pancho Villa

The other muralists – Sequeiros, Orozco, in particular – were equally challenging. Orozco's *The Trench*, at the Escuela Preparatoria, is a powerful image of war and human struggle. On the staircase of the same building, he painted *Cortés y la Malinche*, depicting the naked bodies of the Conqueror and his woman. The painting makes a clear statement about the relationship between Spain and Mexico, between conqueror and conquered, a theme to which Orozco returned many times.

Modern Times

In 1872, the city's population was around 250,000; by 1972 it had exploded to over 15 million and the originally compact urban area had sprawled into the neighboring State of Mexico and over the surrounding mountains. The country's industry was concentrated in the greater Mexico City area, and very few industrial concerns developed outside. While Mexico's peasant population received hardly any benefit from the headlong development, those in the city raised their income substantially and a burgeoning middle class demonstrated how to spend it.

The earthquake of 1985 caused the death of thousands – especially in the slum areas – but the fact that proportionately few of the city's millions of edifices collapsed is a testimony to the skill of Mexican architects and engineers in building structures that could withstand the Richter 8.1 seismic forces. The earthquake also led to the rebuilding of many poorer neighborhoods.

In 1987, downtown Mexico City was declared a Treasure of Humanity by UNESCO and hundreds of historic downtown buildings are now being restored in a flurry of urban-renewal.

The 500th anniversary of Columbus's 'discovery' of America was not celebrated here, as the ghosts of the Conquest have not yet been laid to rest. A consciousness has developed of the value of Indian cultures and there is a newfound pride in what the Aztecs achieved, not least as a result of the accidental unearthing of the huge sculpture of the goddess Coyolxauhqui in 1978 and subsequent excavations of the Main Temple, which have brought to light thousands of pieces of art and artifacts, some of great beauty. Young people with feathered headdresses have taken to dancing in the vicinity of the Main Temple. Perhaps a poem written by an unknown Aztec states the simple truth: 'México-Tenochtitlán endures!'

Modern-day Aztec

Historical Highlights

10,000BC Human settlements in the Valley of Mexico.

600BC Round pyramid is built at Cuicuilco ceremonial center south of present-day Mexico City.

AD1325 Aztecs found Tenochtitlán, their capital, on swampy island in Lake Texcoco. Immediately begin construction of Main Temple Ceremonial Center.

1519 Hernán Cortés and his conquistadors arrive at Tenochtitlán and marvel at island city.

1521 After a 75-day siege, the city falls to the Spanish.

1530 King Carlos V declares Mexico City capital of New Spain and residence of the viceroy.

1553 Founding of the Royal Pontifical University of Mexico.

1571 Inquisition is established in Mexico.

1573 Construction begins on present cathedral.

1592 Site chosen for Alameda Park and first trees planted.

1629 Beginning of five-year flood. Over 30,000 Indians die. Most buildings from the previous century are destroyed.

1785 Founding of the Academia de San Carlos, the first fine arts school on the continent.

1803 Manuel Tolsá finishes bronze equestrian statue of King Carlos IV, popularly known as *El Caballito* (Little Horse).

1810–21 Mexico's War of Independence from Spain.

1846–8 War with the United States. Mexico City invaded. Cadets in military academy in Chapultepec Castle die in battle and are immortalized as the *Niños Héroes* (Boy Heroes). Mexico cedes half its national territory to the US.

1855 President Benito Juárez orders confiscations of Catholic Church property. Separation of Church and State declared.

1864 Maximilian of Hapsburg, sent by Napoleon II to be emperor of Mexico, is received with pomp and ceremony. Executed by firing squad three years later.

1876–1911 General Porfirio Díaz is president, then dictator. His 35-year administration, the *Porfiriato,* is characterized in the capital by European-style architecture and elsewhere by enormous *haciendas* for the few and poverty for the many.

1911–21 Mexican Revolution. Struggle for *Tierra y Libertad* (Land and Liberty). Charismatic leaders Emiliano Zapata and Pancho Villa occupy city for several days in 1910.

1922 Diego Rivera paints *Creation* mural in the Bolívar Amphitheater of the National Preparatory School, thus initiating the Mexican mural movement in art.

1934 *Bellas Artes* theater inaugurated. Art Nouveau façade begun in *Porfiriato,* while interior decorated in Art Deco.

1950 Forty-five-story Latin American Tower built on innovative floating foundations.

1968 Students killed in demonstration in Tlatelolco, days before opening ceremony of the Olympic Games. The first subway line is put into operation.

1985 Earthquake measuring 8.1 on Richter scale strikes city. Thousands killed but most structures are undamaged.

1987 UNESCO designates Historic Downtown Mexico City as a Treasure of Humanity.

1994 North American Free Trade Agreement between Mexico, the US and Canada goes into effect, making the region one of the world's largest trading zones.

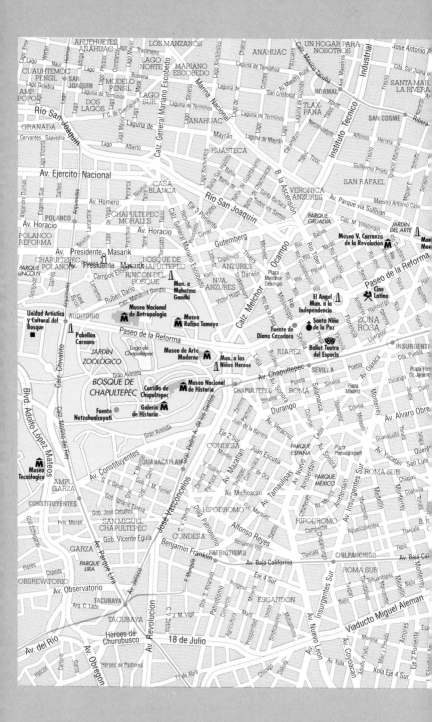

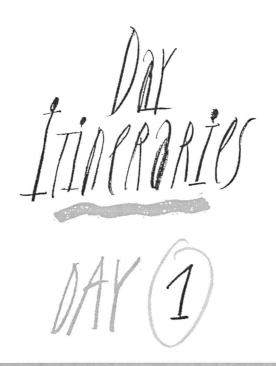

Day Itineraries

DAY (1)

A full day in the historic downtown area, visiting the Zócalo, Diego Rivera murals in the National Palace and the ruins of the Main Temple in the morning, and adjourning to Alameda Park in the afternoon. Dips into the Palacio de Bellas Artes and the Franz Mayer Museum en route. See map on page 21.

—Wear comfortable shoes, as this itinerary involves a lot of walking.—

Begin the day near the Alameda Park and the Palacio de Bellas Artes with breakfast at the charming **Casa de los Azulejos** on Madero Street, a 16th-century house whose distinctive blue and white tile facade was added 150 years ago.

Casa de los Azulejos

It is now well known as **Sanborns** restaurant, but it has been famous at least since the days of Pancho Villa and Emiliano Zapata, whose soldiers insisted on eating here – as recorded in a memorable photograph we will see later. There are several dining areas; be sure to sit in the patio section to savor the striking building.

20

Inside San Francisco church

Afterwards, walk down **Madero**, a bustling street full of typical Mexico City sights and sounds, traffic and noise. The entire heart of the city has been designated as the *Centro Histórico* but it is also jokingly known as the Centro Histérico (Hysterical Downtown). In contrast, there are many stately buildings, both secular and religious, whose interior courts are veritable islands of tranquility amid the hubbub. Just across the street from Sanborns is the **San Francisco church**, visible through an elaborately sculpted stone gateway, once part of an enormous Franciscan monastery founded by Cortés himself, only three years after the Conquest in 1524. The reason for the low level of these buildings is due to the gradual sinking of the church over the centuries, a common phenomenon around town.

The observatory of the **Latin American Tower** (Torre Latino-Americano) affords a panoramic view, though this is sometimes limited by smog. Buy a ticket before taking the elevator (10am–midnight). Looking down on the city below, you will see Alameda Park to the west, with the domed Bellas Artes theater beside it. To the east is the main plaza, cathedral and Aztec ruins.

Continue down Madero, to the **Palacio de Iturbide**, the striking red building at No 17, which boasts remarkable gray stone details and was named after Agustín de Iturbide, who lived here before

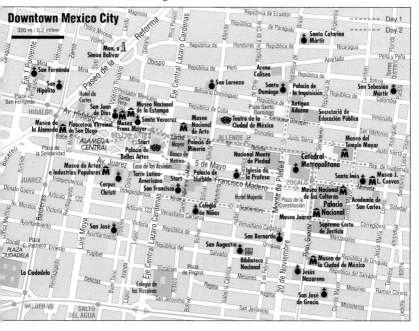

his brief reign as emperor of Mexico in the early 19th century. Art shows are staged in the patio – take a peek to see what's on. A few steps farther on is the **American Bookstore**, a well-stocked purveyor of English-language publications which has been going since the 1920s; the **Librería Britanica** across the street is another good source of reading matter for English speakers. Both of them offer extensive selections of books about Mexico.

Colorful costumes still worn by some Indian cultures in Mexico are on exhibit in the **Museo Serfín** at No 33. Climb the stairs of the **Casasola** photo store at Madero 26. Even if you don't care to pose for a souvenir photo with props from Revolutionary days, you'll enjoy browsing through the shop's prints of old photos from that era, including the one of soldiers dining at Sanborns.

See if you can find the **lion head** embedded in the wall of a building at the corner of Motolinía, which was put there to indicate the level of the devastating floodwaters of 1629. The large church on the left at the corner of Isabel la Católica is **La Profesa**, finished in 1720. Note the bridge spanning a type of dry moat – again the result of the drop in ground level.

At the end of the street is the main plaza or **Zócalo,** a center of civic and religious power since Aztec times. Straight ahead, the long building running along an entire side is the **Palacio Nacional** (National Palace), where the president has his office. To the left is the **Catedral Metropolitana** (cathedral), begun in the 17th century. Its 14 side altars hide in permanent scaffolding, and a pendulum shows how much the building has moved. There is a monument to

The cathedral

Father Bartolomé de las Casas, who fought so hard for Indians' rights in the 16th century, sometimes in opposition to Church policy. The red stone chapel on the right side of the cathedral is the **Sagrario**, which although of a later date than the main building looks older. If you happen to be here at noon on Saturday, you'll witness the bellringing (it lasts for at least 15 minutes).

Cross over to the **National Palace** to view the **Diego Rivera murals** in the stairwell, depicting Mexico from Indian times up to the artist's concept of a future Marxist utopia, reading from right to left and from bottom to top chronologically. Rivera's works are jam-packed with people, the whole cast of history apparently making an appearance. The works upstairs show an idealized view of life in Mexico before the Conquest and the subsequent suffering imposed on the Indians (note his portrayal of villainous Spaniards). The paintings are mostly self-explanatory, but if you would like more detailed information, guides are available upon request on the ground floor.

Rivera mural in the National Palace

For a look at the remains of the Aztec city, proceed to the Main Temple ruins, to the right of the cathedral. On your way, you will pass a metallic scale model of **Tenochtitlán**, complete with water representing Lake Texcoco and pigeon residents. Walk past the bookstores in the buildings to the right to arrive at the last door, which is the entrance to the archaeological site. You may find it's a bit difficult to imagine what it originally looked like, based on what little remains, so it might be more instructive to hire a guide who can bring the bare stones to life. If ruins are not to your taste, proceed directly to the **Museo del Templo Mayor**, where a realistic large model of the ceremonial center in its days of glory can be viewed, together with thousands of pieces found during excavations, many placed on a sand background, like just-discovered treasures. The design of the exhibit is dramatic, with dark walls, low lighting and thick glass panels finely etched with pictures and texts throughout (all in Spanish). The life-sized clay sculptures of warriors are especially impressive.

Depending on the time you have taken to cover this itinerary, cross straight back over the Zócalo to have lunch at the Hotel Majestic's **La Terraza** restaurant overlooking the Zócalo or head behind the cathedral along **República de Guatemala**, observing the different religious goods stores, with their saccharine prints of favorite saints, ornate vestments, golden chalices and statues painted in bright colors. At No 8 is a museum run by the Ministry of Finance exhibiting a collection of colonial paintings. Other options for lunch are **Prendes** (with murals of famous patrons including Gary Cooper and Walt Disney and Mexican politicians, artists, and writers); **El Casino Español** (Spanish food in a palatial setting);

El Rey de Pavo (cheap, clean turkey *tortas*). See the section on *Eating Out* (page 63) for details.

After lunch, take a look at the **Gran Hotel de la Ciudad de México**, around the corner at 16 de Septiembre 82, for its spectacular stained-glass roof, arcaded lobby and turn-of-the-century decor (it was an early form of shopping mall). It is now a Howard Johnson hotel. For the same concept still functioning as a store, cross the street and continue on 5 de Febrero to enter the **Palacio de Hierro** at the corner on the left.

If you'd like to spend the afternoon shopping, consult the *Shopping* section (see page 60) for complete itineraries. If not, El Centro still has much to offer, including the Alameda Park and the Palacio de Bellas Artes and three museums, one of which is the world-class Franz Mayer (make sure you arrive well before closing time at 5pm).

The Gran Hotel

To get to the Alameda Park continue up 16 de Septiembre, noting the many stores in this bustling area. Look up to your left at Palma to see the striking blue and gold mosaic work of the former 'Correo Francés.' Turn left at the corner of Isabel la Católica to admire **Banamex** (a bank's headquarters), which has an extraordinary double staircase. Enter the large red building at No 44 and proceed directly ahead, under the stone arch, and look up. One staircase was for official use and the other was for service: each leads to a different floor.

Back outside, return to 16 de Septiembre, noting the ornate **Casa Boker** at the corner (Sanborns). Continue for half a block to **Casino Español**, at Isabel la Católica 29, built in 1903 in anticipation of a visit by Spanish King Alfonso XIII. When you reach Gante Street, go right two blocks to 5 de Mayo Street; the famous **Cantina La Opera** is on the opposite corner. Check out its turn-of-the-century decor. There are interesting small stores and restaurants on this street, including **El Semillero**, which sells seeds, and the upscale restaurant **L'Heritage**.

By looking down the narrow pedestrian street on the right, you can glimpse the Venetian-inspired architecture of the Correo Mayor (post office) building on the left (covered in more detail in *Day Two*, page 26) and the visibly drooping facade of the Minería building on the right. Many of the structures in this area are bank buildings (mainly Mexico's central bank, Banco de México) and the one at the corner of 5 de Mayo and Eje Central Lázaro Cárdenas merits a look inside for its Art Deco design.

The magnificent white marble Art Nouveau facade of the **Palacio de Bellas Artes** (Fine Arts), with its graceful statues and triple domes, was created at the turn of the 19th century, prior to the Revolution. Its interior, in a totally contrasting, angular Art Deco design, was completed in the 1930s. Upstairs are many murals, including Diego Rivera's re-execution of one he painted in the Rockefeller Center in New York City in the 1930s, which was destroyed. In vengeance, he has portrayed John D Rockefeller being attacked by syphilis germs.

Take a stroll through **Alameda Park**, past the statue of Beethoven and the angel, along the walkways with their inviting benches: this park was once fenced in and admittance was granted only to well-dressed people of Spanish descent. Cross the street at the opposite end, where in the **Museo de la Alameda**, at the corner of Colón and Balderas, you can view Rivera's mural *A Sunday in the Alameda*. It is a satire on the events that have happened in this vicinity, including the burning of heretics in front of the San Diego church next door. The remaining structures of this former monastery, now provide a dignified setting for the **Pinacoteca Virreinal** (Painting Gallery of the Viceroyalty), the most important collection of paintings from the colonial period, when Mexico was governed by a viceroy and was producing the finest art in the Americas.

Now cut back to the park, walking down the back side, along Hidalgo Avenue, and cross at the stop light where you see two churches facing each other on the opposite side. The one on the

Palacio de Belles Artes

left is **San Juan de Dios** and houses a statue of St Anthony, very popular with young women wanting to find husbands.

The church opposite is **Santa Veracruz**. Tucked into the corners of the small **Plaza de la Santa Veracruz** (a perfect example of how the city is sinking) are two museums, the **Franz Mayer** (decorative arts) and the Museo de la Estampa – the former exhibiting antique furniture, paintings, religious sculpture and silver objects collected by Franz Mayer, a German financier who settled in Mexico in the early years of the century. One of the best-designed museums in the country, the Franz Mayer deserves a visit. Don't miss looking into the patio to the left of the lobby, where you can pause to savor a welcome cup of coffee or tea in the beautifully restored cloister.

Back outside, the adjacent **Museo de la Estampa** can be enjoyed for its collection of engravings. Round off the afternoon with a drink in the **Hotel de Cortés,** just up the street at Hidalgo 85, whose sunny and amazingly tranquil patio is an oasis in the midst of the downtown noise and bustle.

Art and Architecture

This full-day itinerary explores aspects of the downtown area not covered on *Day 1*, with special emphasis on art and architecture. It includes the National Museum of Art; the scribes at Plaza Santo Domingo; the San Carlos art school and the Museum of Mexico City. See map on page 21.

–If you want to lunch at the Cicero Centenario as suggested, make a reservation before starting out (tel: 521-29-34).–

Begin this tour at the Palacio de Bellas Artes (covered on *Day 1*). Across the busy street is the **Correo Mayor** (main post office) on Eje Central and Tacuba. Designed by the Italian architect Adamo Oreste Boari and completed in 1906, the exterior is reminiscent of Venetian architecture, while the cavernous interior is packed with stunning detail. Note the beauty of the ironwork throughout. Drop into the postal museum upstairs.

Plaza Manuel Tolsá

Leave via a door onto Tacuba street, continuing a few steps to the right to the charming **Plaza Manuel Tolsá,** in honor of the creator of the enormous equestrian statue facing the **Palacio de Minería**, a neoclassical structure designed by Tolsá and finished in 1813, when Tolsá was professor of sculpture and architecture in the San Carlos Academy. Take a look inside to view its staircase and chapel. Behind the statue is the former Ministry of Communications and Transport, now the **Museo Nacional de Arte**, exhibiting Mexican art from the colonial era up to the present day. An elaborate marble and iron staircase curves up to the first floor where several salons are devoted to the work of Mexico's finest 19th-century landscape painter, José Velasco.

Back outside, cross over to the church on the corner, entering by the side street, to view the collection of the **Museo del Ejercito** (Army Museum), including helmets that look like they might have been worn by the Conquistadors. Continuing down Tacuba, drop in for a cup of coffee and snack at the **Café Tacuba** at No 28, which has been open since 1912, and shouldn't be missed. Note its vaulted ceilings, large paintings, tile wainscoting, amusing backroom mural of nuns having a fast lunch, all of which create the atmosphere of Old Mexico. Stay on the same street until you reach Palma, then turn left one block to continue towards the Zócalo via Donceles to check out the series of stores selling old books, their large stock arranged by subject, with bookish student types in attendance.

Go ahead for one block to República de Brasil and turn left to reach the **Plaza Santo Domingo**, one block away. Take a stroll under the arcade to see the vestiges of a once thriving business here: scribes writing letters for the illiterate or for people needing typed documents. The **Santo Domingo church** was built in the 18th century. The building to its right, with its corner cut off, is the for-

Posing on the plaza

mer **Palacio de la Inquisición**, which housed this now infamous church organization until 1820, when Mexico won its independence from Spain and the Mexican government suppressed the Inquisition. The building later became the School of Medicine and is now the site of the Museum of Mexican Medicine. Next door is the **Antiguo Aduana** (Customs Building), where all the mercantile operations in New Spain were controlled through a Royal Court.

Retrace your steps to turn right on República de Cuba for lunch at a very special place, **Cicero Centenario**, at No 79. This very popular spot, with its lovely decor, whose almost Proustian sense of detail is worthy of *Architectural Digest*, will restore your spirits. Don't miss seeing its diminutive Salón Colibrí (Hummingbird Room), which is just the right size for a romantic dinner for two. Afterwards, if you're a mural fan, two buildings close at hand will interest you: the **Secretaría de Educación Pública** on the corner of Rep de Cuba (which changes its name to González Obregón) and Rep de Argentina, which contains works by Diego Rivera entitled the *History and Life of the Mexican People*, created from 1923 to 1928, and the **Anfiteatro de Bolívar** in the former Escuela Nacional Preparatoria at San Ildefonso No 43, where Diego Rivera began the Mexican muralist movement in 1922, with this work entitled *The Creation*.

Buy a blessing

If murals aren't your thing, continue on Justo Sierra anyway, taking in the many shops in which religious pictures hang next to scantily-clad buxom beauties, and turn right at El Carmen, where there is a profusion of stores selling beauty products, shining costume jewelry and miscellaneous goods. Continue to Moneda, where a right turn will lead you to the **Museo Nacional de las Culturas**, an anthropological museum covering many of the world's cultures. At the end of the street turn right for a few steps to enter the **Escuela Nacional de Artes Plásticas**, better known as La Academia de San Carlos, the oldest art school in the Americas, founded in 1787. Drop in to see the large plaster copies of classic sculpture masterpieces in the majestic patio (Michelangelo's *Moses*, the *Victory of Samothrace*, among others) and generally enjoy the atmosphere of this art school.

Back outside on Academia Street, walk to the next block to the right to visit the **Museo José Luis Cuevas**, at No 13, which is housed in an imaginative restoration of a former convent and exhibits

Anfiteatro de Bolívar

works by this famous Mexican artist, who is still working today. The church on the corner is **Santa Inés** and was part of the convent complex where the Cuevas museum is now located. Retrace your steps on **Moneda** to reach the Zócalo, enjoying this old street and its view of the cathedral framed at the other end.

Rounding the far corner of the cathedral, turn left, walking along the side of the square to reach the large building at the corner of 5 de Mayo, the **Nacional Monte de Piedad** or the National Pawnshop, which was founded by Pedro Romero de Terreros in 1774. In addition to helping people in need, it contains stores, each devoted to a specialty merchandise, ranging from tools to antiques.

If you still have energy and it's early enough (well before 5pm) walk along the left side of the plaza, along the Palacio Nacional, to view the remains of a canal, located at the far end of the palace on Corregidora, a few steps to the left. Although it's hard to imagine, Mexico City was once like Venice. Retrace your steps to reach Pino Suárez Street, passing by the large Suprema Corte de Justicia (Supreme Court) building, and then take a left for a block and a half to the **Museo de la Ciudad de México** (Mexico City Museum), at No 30, for an overview of the city's history from the time of the first human settlements up to the present and a peek into the studio of the Mexican painter Joaquín Clausell, a disciple of the French Impressionists, who worked here in the early 20th century.

Gathering in the Zócalo

PICK & MIX

This Pick and Mix section includes two further tours within Mexico City ('Chapultepec Park and Zona Rosa' and 'San Angel and Coyoácan') and a range of excursions into the surrounding region to see Tula, the ancient capital of the Toltec empire; the temples and pyramids of Teotihuacán; colonial Puebla; the Friday market and volcano at Toluca; and the pretty silver-mining town of Taxco. Except for 'Taxco and Cuernavaca' all the out-of-town excursions can be covered in one day and you can drive, take a regular bus or special tour. (Check at your hotel or consult *Useful Information* in the *Practical Information* section for tour agencies.)

1. Chapultepec Park and Zona Rosa

This full-day tour begins with breakfast at the Camino Real Hotel and moves on to 'museum mile' in Chapultepec Park. The option of spending an hour or so at the zoo is followed by a choice of venues for lunch and a leisurely stroll through the vibrant Zona Rosa.

The **Hotel Camino Real**, two blocks off Reforma on Mariano Escobedo, is a treat to visit. Designed by the renowned architect Ricardo Legorreta in the 1960s, it invites wandering through its generous horizontal spaces to find lobbies, bars, restaurants in inimitable, colorful settings, a perfect example of what has been de-

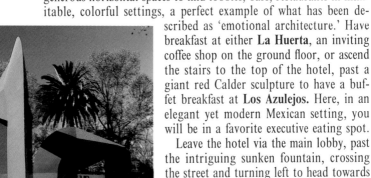

scribed as 'emotional architecture.' Have breakfast at either **La Huerta**, an inviting coffee shop on the ground floor, or ascend the stairs to the top of the hotel, past a giant red Calder sculpture to have a buffet breakfast at **Los Azulejos.** Here, in an elegant yet modern Mexican setting, you will be in a favorite executive eating spot.

Leave the hotel via the main lobby, past the intriguing sunken fountain, crossing the street and turning left to head towards Reforma and a selection of four easy-to-find museums within walking distance of each other. The **Museo de Arte Moderno** is the first, a pair of sleek, glass-sheathed

Sculpture at the Museo de Arte Moderno

Chapultepec Castle

round buildings across the street, with four generously sized exhibition rooms for interesting temporary shows, plus a permanent exhibit of Latin American artists. Take a look into the bookstore, which is packed with a good selection of art publications in Spanish and English.

Take the train or make the 20-minute climb to the **Castillo de Chapultepec** (Chapultepec Castle). The view over the city from the top of the hill is worth the walk and the period artifacts of the **Museo Nacional de Historia** housed here, including the carriage of Maximilian and the bedroom furniture of his wife Carlotta, bring the past to life. The museum's holdings cover events from the Conquest to the Revolution.

The entrance to the castle is a few steps to the left of the gate of the Museo de Arte Moderno on Reforma. You must walk into the park itself, skirting the six-columned **Monumento a Los Niños Héroes** (Boy Heroes) in honor of the cadets who allegedly committed suicide by jumping to their death from the castle wrapped in the Mexican flag, rather than surrender to US forces, who captured the city in 1847.

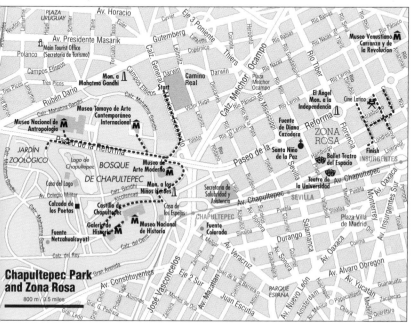

Chapultepec Park and Zona Rosa

800 m / 0.5 miles

In Chapultepec Park

If your energies are limited you might want to skip the castle and proceed directly to the **Museo Nacional de Antropología** (National Anthropological Museum), one long block up the other side of Reforma. The seemingly unfinished blocklike statue standing outside the museum is of Tlaloc, the rain god. It was brought here in the 1960s amid continuous downpours, which some said was his protest at being moved from his original location. The museum's magnificent inside court of pink stone was inspired by the Mayan ruins at Uxmal, specifically the so-called Nunnery Quadrangle.

The striking roof canopy with water falling like rain around the single supporting column is a marvel of engineering. The museum was designed by Mexico's most renowned architect, Pedro Ramírez Vázquez, who was also responsible for the Museo de Arte Moderno, the Aztec Soccer Stadium and other landmarks. A walk around the 11 downstairs halls, beginning with the first on your right, designated as *Introducción a la Antropología,* will provide an overview of all the major pre-Hispanic cultures of Mexico. Some pieces not to be missed are the Aztec calendar stone and the architectural model and painting of Tenochtitlán as it was prior to the Conquest, on exhibit in the Mexica hall at the opposite end of the court.

Multilingual guides are available in the lobby, near the door into the patio, but they cover only one or two of the rooms. If you are an archaeological/anthropological enthusiast, take a quick run around the entire ground floor and return to request a tour of the areas that most intrigued you.

Living cultures can be seen upstairs with authentically costumed mannequins in realistic environments

Statue of Haaxltca

of present-day Mexican villages. Most people find they reach a saturation point after a couple of hours touring the museum, so if you have time, it might be more rewarding to return another day to revisit the sections you liked most. There are video cassettes available just inside the lobby when you exit the patio, some in English, covering different aspects of Mexican history and culture. After touring the museum, your appetite will probably be whetted for information which can be taken in at your leisure, when you return home.

Depending on your tastes, either have lunch at the museum cafeteria down the wide stairway by the Mayan room and continue to the Tamayo Museum or the zoo afterwards, or, if you want a change of pace, proceed directly to the Zona Rosa, where there is a wide range of eating possibilities.

The **Museo Tamayo** next to the Anthropology Museum, just down Reforma, heading back towards downtown, houses the personal collection of the painter Rufino Tamayo in an angular modern setting, with single works by Picasso, de Kooning, Rothko, Warhol and others.

The **zoo** in Chapultepec Park, across the street, can be approached by a nearby entrance. Its prized pandas are exhibited in an air-conditioned environment and the zoo has a proud record of successfully breeding this endangered species. Many other mammals, reptile and bird species can also be seen.

Take a minibus or taxi from across the street to reach the **Zona Rosa**, getting off in front of the Cine Latino movie theater. Landmarks to look for on the way are the **Fuente de Diana Cazadora** (the Diana fountain) and the tall **Angel** monument, which is half a block from where you'll get off. Proceed by Genova Street into this once exclusive but still popular shopping/restaurant area, where you will have a wide choice of restaurants for lunch: **La Gondola** for Italian; **Pizza Real** a few steps further on; and **Konditori**, for pricey but tasty Danish open-faced sandwiches.

Copenhague, a narrow pedestrian street a short block down Hamburgo, is filled with open-air restaurants, with indoor service if you prefer.They include **Piccadilly Pub** for English/American and **La Mesón del Perro Andaluz,** Mexican/Spanish (it has two establishments — one for meat and another for seafood); **La Mansión**, Argentinian steaks, to mention just a few. There are several dining choices in every block of this neighborhood, these are only a handful of the options available within about a two-block area. You might prefer browsing around the streets before making your selection. Local residents go to the **Zona** specifically for eating,

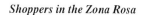
Shoppers in the Zona Rosa

shopping and people-watching and, since long lunches are a Mexican institution, take your time and unwind.

Check out Amberes Street, as exclusive now as it was in the 1960s. You will find jewelry and watches in **Cartier**; casualwear in **Aca Joe**, **Polo** and **Esprit**; religious antiques in **Connoisseur** and don't miss the whimsical, tinted sculptures and jewelry of **Sergio Bustamante**, a Mexican artist of Indian and Chinese origin, who studied architecture before turning to his specialty. **Gucci** is at the corner of Hamburgo; **Los Castillo** has intriguing silver inlay chinaware, among many other original and finely executed designs. The entrance to the glitzy **Plaza Rosa** mall is across the street. Walk around the shops, some of which are packed with goods with a single theme. By turning to the right at VIPS restaurant and walking up Londres, you will find the **Plaza Angel**, a mall specializing in antiques. Its central patio and walkways are filled on Saturday mornings with a popular flea market. Across the street is the **Mercado Insurgentes**, whose persistent but friendly salesmen should not deter you from inspecting the extensive array of silverware, sarapes, embroidered clothing and all kinds of other souvenirs. One side of the market is totally devoted to a series of cheap and clean food counters.

The Zona is a fun place to visit and there's a lot to see, if you enjoy browsing around. The street names are the Spanish translation of European cities: for example, Londres (London), Varsovia (Warsaw), Estocolmo (Stockholm), and so on. Developed at the turn of the 20th century, partially by Americans, it was an exclusive residential neighborhood in its heyday, a place where many embassies were located and wealthy foreigners, as well as Mexican high society, built an eclectic array of mansions. At the time, anything foreign was the vogue, so the area had a cosmopolitan atmosphere right from the start. The present Zona Rosa section was mostly developed in the 1920s and was less exclusive than the neighborhood across Insurgentes. However, its proximity to Reforma, once the most elegant address in the capital, led to its eventual success as a commercial area.

2. San Angel and Coyoacán

Back to the flavor of the colonial period in the once independent towns of San Angel, with its cobblestoned streets and intimate plazas, and Coyoacán, a favorite haunt of artists and intellectuals, with its cafes and bookstores.

Saturday is the best day for visiting **San Angel**, since it's the day of the Bazar Sábado (Saturday Bazaar), a major attraction, together with the art show in the park in front. Any day, however, is fine for enjoying the area's stately yet lovely architecture.

Have breakfast at your hotel before setting out. Take a San Angel bus straight down busy Insurgentes Avenue, telling the driver you want to go to San Angel (*sahn áhn-hel*). The minibus is an experience in itself, with the driver often playing tapes of his favorite music. Designed for maneuverability, these buses seem able to turn on a dime and the drivers take advantage of it, so

Poliforum Cultural de Siqueiros

hold on tight. If this type of adventure is not to your liking, take a taxi, making sure that the meter is running. By bus the trip takes between 45 minutes and 1 hour, by taxi 20–30 minutes.

Landmarks to watch for on the way include the **World Trade Center** (originally the Hotel de Mexico), an office with a revolving restaurant on top set in a park on the right; and the **Poliforum Cultural de Siqueiros**, a faceted building covered in dramatic murals by Siqueiros, which is on the same block and partially enclosed

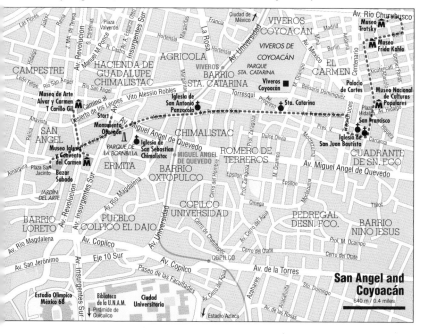

Blooms and bouquets at the flower market

by a murralled fence at the corner. You might like to return here to take a closer look at *The March of Humanity,* said to be the largest mural in the world. On the left about halfway to San Angel is **Liverpool**, a very large 1960s modern department store building next to the **Galerías Insurgentes** shopping center and with a large Longines clock set into its wall.

About 10 blocks ahead, note the mosaic facade, Mexican mural-style (ie, lots of people), of the **Teatro Insurgentes** on the right. Its theme is the theater in Mexico and the work – created by Diego Rivera – is characterised by enormous hands with striking bright red fingernails that appear to hold up the composition. Get off the bus, some 10 blocks after this, at the second Pemex gas station on the right where there's a Sanborns and a park. The large monument across the street is dedicated to Alvaro Obregón, a hero of the Mexican Revolution who was assassinated on this very spot in 1928.

Turn up the side street, Avenida de la Paz, for a walk up to Avenida Revolución. There's a side entrance to **Sanborns** basement store, **La Carreta**, which offers a wide selection of Mexican crafts. Back outside, continue up past **Los Irabien,** a restaurant invisible from the street but full of original paintings and the sound of live piano music, which is a possibility for supper later, as is **Cluny,** almost on the corner, which specializes in French food and has a cozy Art Nouveau atmosphere. Next door is **Ombu,** serving Argentinian food and part of the attractive red-brick **Centro Comercial Plaza de Carmen**, which has three levels of shops.

When you reach the corner of Avenida Revolución, you have a choice of visits: first, the **Museo del Carmen**, in the blue-and-yellow-tile-domed church to your left. Formerly a Carmelite monastery that now exhibits religious paintings and objects, it has an attractive small cloister downstairs with fruit trees and, if you care to see them, mummified bodies of monks and nuns in the basement. Your

second option is to turn right and visit the **flower market**, not so much for its exotic blooms but to observe the curiously stiff geometric flower arrangements that are a specialty. If you visit during the week you could also tour the modern **Museo de Arte Alvar y Carmen T Carrillo Gil** at the corner of Revolución and Desierto de los Leones, one long block ahead. It exhibits works by major 20th-century painters including Diego Rivera, Orozco, and Siqueiros, and has temporary exhibitions. Perhaps you'll want to visit all three places, depending on your stamina. However, if it's Saturday, the goings on at the Plaza San Jacinto are not to be missed.

Back at the corner of Revolución and Av de la Paz, cross the street, and proceed towards the compact park, walking up the right-hand side. The inviting corner created by the stately surrounding houses, one of which is the **Biblioteca de la Revolución** (Library of the Revolution), is called **Plaza del Carmen** and is a pleasant gateway into San Angel. Further along (you're now on Amargura Street), the sculptural forms of the dignified old houses set flush with the sidewalk and the occasional glimpse of a lush garden through a gate will begin to cast their spell and by the time you reach the end of the street, where a small, red building (now an advertising agency) blocks the straight path, you will know why the area is so popular with overwrought *capitalinos* nostalgic for a quieter time.

Turn left to reach the **Plaza San Jacinto**. If it's Saturday, the whole area will be filled with people, some selling and others browsing and buying. Start with a reconnaissance of the upscale **Bazar**

Sábado, whose entrance is the first door to the left. The salespeople are often selling their own handiwork, which ranges from the quaint and cheap to the grand and expensive – delicate wooden Madonnas with ethereal long-fingered hands; jewelled crosses straight out of a Byzantine fantasy; sculptures that fit on the end of a toothpick and have to be seen through a magnifying glass.

There is a buffet restaurant in the sunny patio and another restaurant inside at the back that's dim and cozy by comparison.

Buy a basket?

Two other lunch possibilities right on the plaza are: **La Casona del Elefante**, to the left of the bazaar, serving Indian food, and the **Fonda San Angel**, a few doors further down, offering tasty Mexican cooking; both offer inside and outside tables.

Casa Risco's fountain

Portraits from the 16th, 17th and 18th centuries are on permanent exhibit at the **Casa Risco** museum next door. Even if you don't go upstairs to see the paintings, duck into the patio to see the eccentric fountain backdrop: the wall is embedded with seashells and plates and there are even chinaware columns created by stacking up Oriental cups. The whole composition is topped off by a majolica statue of a blond Samson wrestling with a dog-like lion.

Stroll around the plaza itself, filled on Saturdays with paintings and engravings in many sizes, styles and prices. On the far side are stalls with a variety of objects – one of my favorites is the *palo de lluvia* ('rain pole'), which is said to be a pre-Hispanic musical instrument made out of a length of hollow bamboo. Tiny pegs are hammered into it and a supply of small stones added – when upended, you hear a sound like falling rain. There is a stone plaque on a wall halfway around the plaza, opposite the bazaar honoring members of the St Patrick's brigade, composed of Irish soldiers fighting with the US forces under General Zachary Taylor, that occupied the city in 1847. Under the influence of a local Catholic priest, they deserted to fight on the side of Mexico and were later executed here by the Americans. There are around 75 names listed, some of them clearly not Irish. Underneath is a text which translates: 'With the gratitude of Mexico 112 years after their sacrifice, September 1959.'

The small plaza on the side of the bazaar is full of even more *artesanías*. Walking past it, you will come upon the **San Jacinto church** on the left, one of the most popular churches for weddings – its verdant atrium is perfect for warm congratulations after the ceremony. Sometimes you can even see a wedding traffic jam, with one wedding party embracing in the garden after Mass, another inside getting married and a third waiting its turn. Continue farther on to the small crossroads of Reina, Hidalgo, Arbol and Juárez streets to understand why San Angel is such a desirable residential address. Some of the most beautiful houses in Mexico are hidden behind the high walls.

Retrace your steps, enjoying the street from a different angle, on the way to the taxi stand next to the Fonda San Angel for a fast and comfortable transfer to **Coyoacán** (a 15-minute drive). Already a town in pre-Hispanic times, Coyoacán was near the shore of Lake Texcoco. Cortés set up his government here after the conquest and destruction of Tenochtitlán and remained until the city had been made ready for Spanish residence, two years later. Still a separate entity

in the 1940s, it was home to many celebrities – Frida Kahlo, Diego Rivera, Leon Trotsky, actress Dolores del Río – and it remains a desirable neighborhood for bohemians and artists as well as the wealthy.

Be sure to tell the taxi driver to enter Coyoacán by **Avenida Francisco Sosa** or, if your Spanish is very limited, write down Coyoacán via Francisco Sosa. The reason for taking this specific route is so you'll see one of the most beautiful streets in the city on your way. When you see a siena-colored double arch at the end of the street, get out of the car and walk the last couple of blocks, to savor the shade of the tall trees and the flavor of the colonial houses. On the left you may see dancers practicing through the open windows of **Los Talleres,** a cultural center.

Going through the arch, you enter the first of two adjacent plazas, **Jardín Centenario**. The fountain with coyotes playing in the center is in honor of the Nahuatl name Coyohuacan, which means the Place of the Coyotes. On weekends, the area is abuzz with activity: spontaneous live theater; street musicians; numerous stands where peddlers sell handmade jewelry and clothing; browsers leafing through books arranged on a low table; a lone cassocked priest on his way to or from the cathedral, and families just enjoying the slower pace of the area. There are several sidewalk cafes along one side of the plaza; the eatery outside **El Parnaso** bookstore, a great vantage point for people-watching, is a favorite hangout with intellectuals. There is a **Sanborns** on the opposite side of the square, with an attractive restaurant and bar upstairs. During the week, the plaza seems like the heart of a sleepy provincial town.

The large imposing church is **San Juan Bautista**. Walk past it into the second square, **Plaza Hidalgo**, noting the ornate bandstand, the sculptured tree trunk, and the **Palacio Municipal** building on the left. At the end of the plaza, continue ahead on the street beside the *panadería* (bakery), heading to the **Museo Nacional de**

Outdoor theater-goers in Coyoacán

Self-portrait by Frida Kahlo

Culturas Populares, a few steps ahead on Hidalgo, where temporary exhibits focus on how people from contemporary cultures live.

Back outside, go back to the corner, turning left for a short block alongside the plaza and take the first left on Higuera to visit the tiny market just a couple of doors down where, if you're lucky, you will find an unusually artistic **pancake maker** who has set up shop in front of a fantasy castle set. He dribbles batter from a spoon with the precision of a draftsman, creating Disney characters for children and shapely girls for older patrons. Pop in to see if he's at work. If you're in the mood for a drink in a Mexican cantina, continue a few steps on to **La Guadalupana.**

Now, prepare to trek around eight blocks to the **Museo Frida Kahlo**, at the corner of Londres and Allende, where the painter was born and later lived with Diego Rivera. To get there, retrace your steps to the plaza and continue in the direction of the bakery, continuing alongside the square until you reach the beginning of Allende. You'll pass by the famous Coyoacán market on the way. Frida's blue house, some six streets ahead at Londres 247 is suffused with her character – the Mexican kitchen has her name and Diego's on the wall in an arrangement of small clay cups.

The **Trotsky Museum** is about six blocks away at Río Churubusco 410 (leave the Frida museum, going left, and continue on Londres until you reach Morelos, taking another left for two blocks). Trotsky's house is presently painted a yellowish color and has bricked-up windows. Proceed to the corner and turn left. This rather eerie, austere building, with its small garden, collection of books in several languages, bedroom with strong metal doors and window shutters, impresses the visitor as a refuge that, in the end, did not protect the refugee.

The nearest Metro stations are a short taxi-drive away. Ask to go either to Coyoacán or Zapata or else walk back to the center of Coyoacán, where there are a variety of buses available.

You could wind up the day with supper at **San Angel Inn**, located at Palmas No 50 in the San Angel area. This former *hacienda* retains the charm and aristocratic air of a bygone era and you will dine to the sound of strolling guitarists singing romantic songs.

A full-day excursion combining the rich splendor of the Jesuit monastery of Tepotzotlán with the ancient site of Tula, capital of the Toltec empire. See map on page 42.

See map on page 42.

The former Jesuit seminary and monastery of **Tepotzotlán** is just north of the city, via the road to Querétaro. From the center of Mexico City, proceed west by Reforma, past the Auditorio Nacional, taking a right at the Fuente de los Petróleos, heading towards Satellite City. Several miles farther on, continue past the giant sculptural group of four painted modern towers, and the commercial zone, until you have left the urban area behind. The turn off to Tepotzotlán is about 32km (20 miles) away.

Head to the center of the small town, getting out near the church with its single tower. Even the elaborate facade, considered one of the most beautiful in Mexico, belies the glories that await within. The name Tepotzotlán means 'Place of the Hunchback' in the Nahuatl language and was an Otomí Indian settlement prior to the arrival of the Spaniards. The Jesuits came here in the 16th century, establishing a seminary for aristocratic Indians which lasted on and off until the present century.

The magnificent **church** interior reached its present splendor in the 18th century and is breathtaking in the complexity and richness of its gold altarpieces, paintings, sculptures and chapels. It would take an annotated diagram to figure out exactly what is going on in the extraordinarily complex compositions of the retables, but suffice to say that the symbolism of the figures represented centers on Jesuit themes, with Jesuit characters, plus the usual saints and Madonnas – some executed in sculpture in the round and others in paintings by masters of Mexican colonial art, such as Miguel Cabrera and Cristóbal de Villalpando. The magnificent chapel named the

The ornate interior of the church at Tepotzotlán

Museo Nacional del Virreinato

Camerino, meaning 'dressing room,' is literally that, the place where statues of the Virgin Mary are vested with different robes, selected in accordance to events in the Church calendar, as is the custom in Mexico. In the past, one unkind way to describe the life of an old maid here was to say, 'She ended up dressing holy statues.'

This architectural style, known as *churrigueresque*, is Mexican in a very distinctive way. The architect Guillermo García-Oropeza who regards Tepozotlán as a masterpiece, has described it as a genuine, native product with its 'lavish use of color and movement, in its excesses and in its unbounded imagination.' Baroque goes well with Mexican sensitivity, he writes, speculating that 'perhaps Mexicans at heart are a baroque people, helplessly in love with color, with murals, with ornament. In them lives a fantasy that often verges on the surreal.'

Despite the luxury, this was once a functioning seminary so be sure to visit the monastery section, which now houses an important collection of colonial painting, ivories and other works of art in the **Museo Nacional del Virreinato** (National Museum of the Viceroyalty). Wander through the halls, into the colonial kitchen to imagine monk cooks hard at work, and stroll in the peaceful orchard and garden in the back.

Every Christmas, special Christmas plays called *Pastorelas* are performed at Tepotzotlán. They seem to be a continuation of the medieval theater tradition.

Before setting out for Tula, enjoy lunch at one of Tepotzotlán's attractive restaurants, as refreshments are not abundant at the archaeological site.

Some 31km (50 miles) further north on the Querétaro highway are the ruins of the city of **Tula** (an 80-minute bus ride from Mexico City's northern bus terminal). Tula (from the Nahuatl word *Tollan*: 'the place of reeds'), flourished as the capital of the Toltec empire from the late 10th to the 12th century, between the fall of Teotihuacán and the rise of the Aztec Tenochtitlán. It may have reached a population of 50,000. Today, little remains – even the Aztecs are said to have carried away parts of the site to their own city. The ancient site is just over 2km (1 mile) from the rather colorless town of Tula itself. If you arrive by bus you'll have to walk or take a taxi.

Be sure to visit the **museum** at the entrance for an overview of what was once here. Tula is the home of the mythical **Quetzalcoatl**, the priest god, who became one of the most important in the Mesoamerican pantheon. He was said to have left Tula in shame, after being induced to get drunk by his enemies and, in his intoxication, engaging in sexual relations with his sister. He eventually reached the Yucatán, where he is also a god but known as Kukulkán. Among the many accounts of the story is one which maintains that he departed forever by sea and another in which he burned himself to death, returning as the morning star. Near the entrance of the site is **Ball Court No 1** (the second has not yet been fully excavated), a type of structure seen at many sites with Toltec influence. Another Toltec characteristic is the colonnade at the base of the main pyramid, which greatly resembles those at Chichen Itzá in the distant Yucatán peninsula. This pyramid, known by the name of **Temple of the Morning Star** or **Quetzalcoatl Pyramid** is memorable because of the enormous 4.5-m (15-ft) **Toltec warrior columns** standing on top – equipped with spear throwers in one hand, a small sword in the other and bearing a stylized butterfly emblem (a Toltec symbol) on their chests. There are more square columns behind these, where the altar may have been located but it is not known whether there was a roof on top or not. Along the north wall of the pyramid is the **serpent wall** or Coatepantli, a relief sculpture showing snakes devouring human skeletons.

Adjacent is the **Palacio Quemado** (Burnt Palace), which was originally composed of several halls. Some wall paintings of nobles can still be seen. The partially visible **Main Temple** is in front of these struc-

Toltec warrior

Coatepantli, Tula

tures to the right and the second ball court is to the left. Tula was not excavated until the 1940s and only definitively identified as the site of the Toltec capital in the 1970s.

Those continuing on to San Miguel de Allende will pass through colonial **Querétaro**, a key city in Mexican history, where the War of Independence from Spain began in the early 1800s, Emperor Maximilian was executed in 1867 and the present national constitution was written in 1916. The city is famous for its pink stone aqueduct, former convents and other old buildings.

4. Teotihuacán and Guadalupe Basilica

A full-day excursion to see the pyramids, palaces and temples of Teotihuacán, the largest archaeological site in Mexico, and returning via the Basilica of Guadalupe. See map on page 42.

—Be prepared for a lot of walking when visiting the pyramids at Teotihuacán. If you decide to go via public transportation, the bus takes about an hour from the Northern Bus Terminal Autobuses del Norte Metro station Indios Verdes. Take something to eat and bottled water with you and tuck your camera away in your bag.—

Teotihuacán was the most important city state of the Classic era whose apogee was from AD200–500. Spread over an area larger than ancient Rome at its height, it had a population of perhaps 200,000 and a sphere of influence reaching far into Central America. There is no historical record of this people. Even the name **Teotihuacán** (meaning place of the gods) was given to the site by the Aztecs, as

were most of the other designations still in use today, such as the Pyramid of the Sun, the Pyramid of the Moon and the Avenue of the Dead. When the Aztecs visited around the year 1200, the city had already been abandoned for hundreds of years. The impressive central avenue as we now see it had not even been fully excavated before the 1960s. Until then it looked like a dusty path lined with mounds of earth which hid the platforms beneath.

Despite the lack of written records, the excavations have revealed some fascinating data: there was city planning, based on a grid layout; drainage systems for water; well laid out 'apartment' complexes; dif-

Teotihuacán relic

Ornamental knife seller in front of the Pyramid of the Moon

ferent neighborhoods for the various artisans and foreigners and evidence of far-reaching trade. The date of the fall of the city is estimated at around AD700, about two centuries before the Mayan cities were abandoned. Another theory, adding to the many explaining why the Mayans deserted their cities, is that the demise of Teotihuacán, the most important metropolis and religious center in Mesoamerica, may have demoralized the other peoples, leading to a loss of faith and rejection of their gods, shown by the abandonment of their places of worship.

Begin with the **museum** near the entrance to get a general orientation before proceeding to the ruins themselves. You will have to pay an extra fee as you enter the ruins for any camera that the ticket-takers notice. If you want to concentrate on the main pyramids and avoid the trek up the nearly 3-km (1½-mile) central avenue, proceed to the second entrance near the Pyramid of the Sun. There is a small cafe and snackbar above the museum but no other source of food or

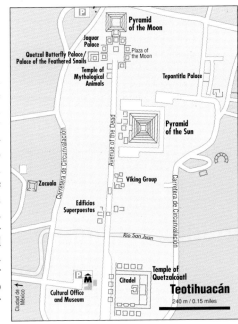

drink on the entire site, so keep your bottle of water or can of soda handy – on a hot day you will be glad of it. In summertime it is often rainy in the afternoons.

Just outside the museum, you will cross the **Avenue of the Dead**, to reach the **Citadel** (misnamed by the Spaniards due to its similarity to a fort), consisting of a plaza enclosed on four sides by temple platforms, one of which is the **Temple to Quetzalcoatl**, one

Fresco in the Jaguar Palace

of the best-preserved examples of Teotihuacán building, with the serpent heads along the staircase. You can get a good idea of the layout of the rest of the city, by looking towards the enormous **Pyramid of the Sun** from the highest point of the temple.

Continuing towards the main pyramids, you will cross a dry riverbed, whose waters once separated the northern part of the city from the south.

The length of the avenue gives some idea of the size of the city and it actually ascends a total of 30m (98ft), so that the much smaller Pyramid of the Moon at the end seems as tall as the Pyramid of the Sun. The latter is one of the greatest achievements of pre-Hispanic architecture, covering an area the size of the Cheops Pyramid in Egypt (though it is not as tall). The entire structure was once covered in stucco and brightly painted.

The pyramid can be ascended by the stairs, but a word of caution – there is no handrail or other support, which can cause problems when coming down.

Back on the Avenue of the Dead, to the left of the Pyramid of the Moon, are three palaces: the **Palacio del Quetzalpapalotl** (Quetzal Butterfly Palace), named after its reliefs of a mythological animal, part quetzal bird and part butterfly, which was a deity often portrayed in Teotihuacán. Next is the **Jaguar Palace** with paintings of stylized jaguars and finally is the **Palacio de los Caracoles Emplumados** (Palace of the Feathered Snails), located below the Quetzalpapalotl Palace, with the best-preserved examples of wall painting at the site. This complex provides a more intimate impression of Teotihuacán's private life, as it was a priests' residence.

Finally, at the end of the avenue, is the **Pyramid of the Moon**, with a plaza in front, surrounded by several platforms. A panoramic view of the entire ceremonial center can be had from this point. One can only imagine how the city must have been in its days of glory – full of the bright colors and bustle of the capital of the most powerful nation of its time. During the 1968 Olympic Games the entire Avenue of the Dead came to life with hundreds of brightly costumed dancers performing on all the platforms.

Pyramid of the Moon

For well-earned refreshment after the exertions of exploring there are several possibilities. Apart from the museum cafe and restaurant (the latter is quite expensive), you might try **Pyramid Charlie's**, which is about halfway between gates 1 and 2 on the cobbled road parallel to the fence, or **La Gruta**, which, as its name says, is in a large, cool cave a 15-minute walk outside the site (signs guide you). Club Med has a hotel and restaurant nearby, the Hotel/Restaurant Villa Arqueológica. All these are on the road encircling the site.

Two other places might be combined with today's tour. Firstly, there's the **Acolman Convent**, a 16th-century fortress-like establishment, whose defensive structure was not due to caprice but to the real possibility of hostility from unconquered Indian tribes. It is located some 10km (6 miles) from the pyramids on the highway back. There are murals inside the church and the cloister.

Secondly, back in Mexico City, not far from La Villa Metro station, is the **Basilica de Guadalupe**, an architecturally unique basilica built to supplement a 16th-century structure famous for its miraculous image of the Virgin Mary. The new, much larger basilica, designed by Pedro Ramírez Vázquez and built in 1976, has been labeled a monstrosity (a moving ramp now carries the faithful past the picture) but it serves its practical purpose of accommodating thousands of people at one time.

This Madonna is the patron saint of Mexico. History states that in 1531 the Virgin appeared to the Indian Juan Diego several times and in her last appearance gave him a gift of roses that were not in season, which he was instructed to carry in his *tilma* (cape) to the bishop. When Juan Diego opened this garment before the bishop, letting the roses fall out, the prelate was astounded to see an image of the Madonna on the *tilma*. It was thus proclaimed of miraculous origin. The image in the church is said to be from the very same garment and is held in great reverence by Mexicans. On December 12, the feast day of the Virgin of Guadalupe, millions of people

from all over Mexico make the pilgrimage to the basilica. There is a small chapel at the top of the hill behind the old church, marking the spot where the apparition took place.

The gardens of the Basilica

5. Puebla

East to Puebla, a colonial gem, with a stop-off in Cholula. See map on page 42.

Whether you decide to travel the 130km (80 miles) to beautiful Puebla by tour bus, regular busline, tourist taxi or hire car, the fastest route to the state capital is via federal highway 150D, a continuation of the thoroughfare Calzada Ignacio Zaragoza which begins near the airport. The road crosses the drab working-class suburb of Netzahualcóytl (population over 2 million), but eventually emerges in a dramatically different landscape of pine forests. Out of these loom enormous snow-capped volcanoes: Ixtaccíhuatl (5,286m/17,342ft), whose Nahuatl name means 'sleeping woman' (which the peak resembles), and the 'smoking mountain,' Popocatépetl (5,452m/

Popocatépetl and Ixtaccíhuatl

17,887ft), which form part of the Sierra Nevada that separates the Valley of Puebla from the Valley of Mexico. Two volcanic peaks on the other side of Puebla are La Malinche (4,450m/14,600ft) and Orizaba (5,654m/18,551ft) – the latter being the highest mountain in Mexico.

Puebla is unusual in that it was founded on a spot where no Indian settlement had previously been established and right from the beginning was set up as a city expressly for Spaniards. The location chosen – on the road from the Gulf coast to Mexico City, the capital of New Spain – was strategic, both from a military and commercial point of view. After Mexico City's disastrous five-year flood of 1629–34 Puebla became more important than the capital. The sudden influx of refugees included many wealthy families.

Puebla's downtown layout can be confusing, even though it follows a strict grid pattern. Taking the Zócalo as the starting point, the streets to the north have even numbers and, with 5 de Mayo as the dividing line, are either west (*Poniente*/Pte) or east (*Oriente*/Ote). To the south, 5 de Mayo changes its name to 16 de Septiembre and the perpendicular streets have odd numbers. Referring back to the Zócalo, the Avenida de la Reforma crosses 5 de Mayo, changing its name to Avenida Ma Camacho afterwards. The streets crossing it to the west are odd-numbered and are either north (*Norte*) or south (*Sur*), while on the other side of 5 de Mayo they become even-numbered.

A major religious center almost from the beginning, the city boasts Mexico's second largest **cathedral**, a rather severe but refined design in the Spanish Renaissance Herreriano style, named after Juan de Herrera whose Escorial palace-monastery near Madrid typifies this type of architecture. Located on the south side of the

The 'portales,' Puebla

main plaza, the cathedral is well worth a visit, to see in particular the choir screen and stalls and the main altar designed by Manuel Tolsá, the creator of Mexico City's El Caballito and Palacio de Minería. Legend has it that the towers are so high that angels had to hang the bells.

The Puebla **Zócalo** is a hub of city activity. The *portales*, the arcaded passageways, are a favorite meeting place, where you can have a leisurely cup of coffee at one of its sidewalk cafes or browse in the stores.

One of the few cities in the country with a large number of colonial buildings in excellent condition, Puebla developed its own architectural style, a light-hearted baroque, with a type of red-brick or terracotta tile facing, generous use of tiles and contrasting white moldings. After viewing the cathedral, cross Av 5 Oriente to visit the former Archbishop's Palace, now the **Casa de Cultura** and the location of the incomparable **Biblioteca Palafoxiana** (Palafoxian library) founded in the 17th century and named after the city's most famous bishop, Juan de Palafox y Mendoza. Entering through the magnificent stone portal, you'll see shelf after shelf of rare books covered in cream-colored vellum, including some of the earliest printed books in Mexico.

Walk to the right on Calle 2 Sur for two blocks to reach the **Museo Amparo** at the corner of Av 9 Oriente, a state-of-the-art institution with interactive computerized explanations in several languages, exhibiting pieces from before the Conquest and the colonial period in a dramatically designed setting. Among the unusual

Biblioteca Palafoxiana

exhibits is a three-dimensional time chart in the form of a mural, showing what was going on in the different continents at a given period in time.

Continue along Av 9 Oriente for a block, past the church **El Templo de la Compañía** where the famous China Poblana is buried. She was said to be an Oriental princess who was sold into slavery and ended up in Puebla, where she reputedly designed the beaded costume considered the city's own (which curiously has nothing Chinese about it). Of greater interest is the **Casa del Alfeñique**, at the corner of 6 Norte and 4 Oriente, with its red facade set off by white decoration looking like the icing on a wedding cake. It houses a museum exhibiting a variety of 18th- and 19th-century pieces and settings, including a Pueblan kitchen, as well as some examples of the famous China Poblana costume.

Selling 'tortillas'

El Parián, the 19th-century market building, is between Av 2 and Av 4 Oriente, and the **Barrio del Artista**, where artists once lived, is nearby. Continue north to the **Teatro Principal**, one of the first theaters in the Americas. Now turn left on 8 Oriente, continuing about four blocks to 5 de Mayo, noting on the way the **Casa de los Hermanos Serdán** – brothers who were early revolutionaries – now an interesting museum of the Mexican Revolution at Av 6 Oriente, No 206. Turn right on 5 de Mayo, heading towards the **Exconvento de Santa Mónica**, at Av 18 Poniente No 103. This institution, with its hidden rooms, continued to operate secretly against laws decreeing the disbanding of convents until 1934 and is now a museum. Take a left for one block, then continue on 3 Norte for about

The kitchen in the Exconvento de Santa Rosa

three blocks to reach the **Exconvento de Santa Rosa**, which is now an arts and crafts museum. The main reason for coming here is to see the magnificent tiled kitchen, where *mole poblano,* the spicy sauce whose ingredients include chocolate and chile, was created.

Down the same street, near 5 Poniente, is one sight you must see, the Iglesia de Santo Domingo's **Capilla del Rosario** (rosary chapel), a 17th-century masterpiece of Mexican baroque architecture which is totally covered with decoration, some gold-leafed. Before returning to the Zócalo, take a left at 2 Poniente to the **Casa de los Muñecos** at 2 Norte, whose typical Pueblan features, such as terracotta and tile facing, are supplemented by ceramic tiles painted with peculiar human figures. One explanation has it that they are the enemies of the original owner.

Retrace your steps to Calle 3 Norte, for the **Museo Bello**, at 3 Poniente, where fine Mexican furniture, paintings and talavera ware adorn the beautifully designed rooms of this former private home. Finally, continue to Av 3 Poniente No 307 to reach the charming **Fonda Santa Clara** restaurant for a wonderful lunch of regional cuisine. In late summer, *chiles en nogada,* a rich dish whose walnut sauce, chile and pomegranate seeds replicate the colors of the Mexican flag, is sure to be on the menu.

For purchasing and/or ordering the typical Pueblan talavera ware, with its brilliant blue, yellow and white colors and high prices, visit **Casa Rugerio**, 18 Poniente 111; **Uriarte**, 4 Poniente 911, or **Fábrica de Azulejos la Guadalupana**, Av 4 Poniente 911.

Although once – around AD800 – the most important city and religious center in central Mexico, **Cholula**, about 10km (6 miles) from Puebla, is today more of a suburb than a separate town. Its heyday was between the fall of Teotihuacán and the rise of Tula, when it was the meeting place of various Mesoamerican cultures. The **Great Pyramid**, which looks like a big, muddy hill topped by a church, is a 10-minute walk along Avenida Hidalgo from where the bus stops. It is the largest structure of its kind in the world. As everywhere else in Mexico, the pyramid was built on top of other pyramids through the centuries. There are stairs up the outside of the pyramid, from the top of which you can enjoy a good view of the city and its many churches. A **museum** at the site contains a cut-away model of the pyramid which is very instructive.

In the 1930s extensive tunnels were dug between pyramid levels and painted surfaces were revealed (there are tours through portions of these underground passages, but anyone who suffers from claustrophobia should avoid going inside.

The reason for such a small town having so many churches is that Cortés vowed to build 365, one for each day of the year, most probably to demonstrate Spanish and Catholic domination over the previous religion. He presumably also wanted to undermine the influence of this major ceremonial center, considered one of the most sacred by different cultures on account of Quetzalcoatl's sojourn here after his exile from Tula, en route to the Yucatán. It is likely that the churches were built on top of Indian temples.

Of the many churches which can be visited, one of the most interesting is the **Convento de San Gabriel**, whose **Capilla Real** is unique in the Americas due to its dozens of domes supported by many columns, inspired by Córdoba's great mosque. Outside is an enormous atrium, where the Indians could hear Mass in the open air (one theory has it that they hesitated to go into a building because they were accustomed to worshipping outdoors, but the reason may have been fear of being rounded up in an enclosed space, after the massacre of over 3,000 of their people by Cortés's men).

For those who love zoos, **Africam**, a park where you can drive among the animals, is some 24km (15 miles) from Puebla to the south on the road to the Laguna de Valsequillo.

6. West to Toluca

An excursion to Toluca, the highest town in Mexico, with the chance to enter the crater of a volcano. This is a good option for Friday, when the weekly market is held. See map on page 42.

—Bus services to Toluca from Mexico City leave from Terminal Central Poniente, which can be reached by taking Metro Line 1 to Observatorio, the last station (the bus terminal is adjacent). The company

Toluca's Friday Market

ETN operates a deluxe service every hour from 7am–11pm and TNT leaves every 5 minutes; both cover the 72-km (45-mile) drive in about an hour. Toluca's bus station is 2km (1 mile) from the town itself.—

If your time in Mexico is very short, it is probably more rewarding to visit Teotihuacán, Puebla and Taxco rather than **Toluca**. However, Toluca, the country's highest city at over 2,590m (8,500ft) and capital of the State of Mexico, is a pleasant place to live, with its university, museum complex, symphony orchestra and small-scale buildings, and it makes a pleasant stop en route to Valle del Bravo or the cities of Morelia and Guadalajara. Its Friday market is an attraction as is the crater of the Nevado de Toluca volcano.

Getting a shoe shine

If you're driving, the most scenic route to the Toluca exit is by Paseo de la Reforma, through the exclusive Lomas de Chapultepec, a residential area developed in the 1930s and 1940s. Two highways lead to Toluca, but the new toll road (designated as 'Cuota') is faster. Both run through pine forests which, though somewhat depleted, are a great relief after the urban concentration of the capital and a surprise to some foreign visitors.

Toluca used to be best known for its Friday **market**, to which Indians come to sell arts and crafts and where farm animals, foodstuffs and manufactured goods are for sale. It is less of an attraction now that it has moved from a downtown location to the Paseo de Tollocán, the wide tree-shaded boulevard that serves as the entryway to the city. For viewing arts and crafts in a calmer setting, visit the **CASART store** at Paseo Tollocán 700.

In recent years, Toluca has stepped up its industrial development and is now the site of major plants. These have brought jobs and significant growth, and the population has now reached around half a million inhabitants, including many *capitalinos* who abandoned Mexico City after the 1985 earthquake.

The city's name derives from the Nahuatl word *tolloacán*, meaning 'the place of reverence.' Prior to the Conquest it was settled by various Indian groups, including the Otomís and Mazahuas, whose ceremonial centers are now archaeological sites (Teotenango and Calixlahuaca).

Toluca's downtown area centers on the arcade next to the **Plaza de los Mártires**, where the famous local drink Los Moscos is sold in **La Miniatura**, an intriguing store that sells it in various strengths, depending on the intended recipient: the strongest is promoted for mothers-in-law. Nearby is **La Purísima**, where curtains of candles are suspended by their wicks, and strings of spicy red and some-

La Purísima

times green sausages, called *chorizo*, one of Toluca's claims to fame, hang in booths outside. There are several restaurants under the arches; **Fonda Rosita** offers tasty Mexican food.

The 19th-century **cathedral**, on the Independencia Street side of the Portales, is disappointingly modern for fans of colonial art but the nearby **Templo del Carmen**, on the other side of the twin plazas, is attractive. Don't miss looking into the **Museo de Bellas Artes**, in a former convent adjoining the Carmen church, with its small patio in a refined classic style. The **Museo de Numismática**, at Bravo Norte 303 and Lerda, exhibits Mexican coins in a diminutive house. Nearby at the corner of Lerdo de Tejada and Benito

Juárez is the **Cosmovitral Botánico**, the home of the Friday market until the mid-1970s, and now the site of a botanical garden. Its brilliantly colored stained-glass panels tell the story of humanity and the cosmos.

On the edge of town is the **Centro Cultural Mexiquense**, located on land that was part of the former Hacienda de la Pila, a cultural center comprising four museums and a library in a lovely setting, with tree-covered hills close

Cosmovitral Botánico

at hand and the snow-capped volcano in the distance. The **Popular Arts Museum** is in the original residence and offers a selection of local crafts, including the exquisite Temoaya carpets fashioned out of silky wool. The enormous Tree of Life sculptures were created on the spot. The **Museum of Modern Art** boasts easel paintings by several 20th-century Mexican masters; the **Museum of Anthropology**'s holdings range from pre-Hispanic archaeological pieces to modern-day items. There is a **Charro Museum**, displaying the accessories and equipment of the traditional Mexican horsemen. Rounding out the cultural complex is the **Library**.

About 16km (10 miles) from the city (branch off Highway 55) is the **Zacango Zoo**, which has tigers, elephants, giraffes, etc, most seemingly content in their cool highland surroundings.

If you'd like to enter the mouth of a volcano (inactive), drive around 80km (50 miles) on the road to Sultepec to reach the **Nevado de Toluca**, whose name in the original Nahuatl is the tongue-twisting *Xinantécatl*. You can actually drive into the crater to view the two lakes at the bottom, called Lake of the Sun and Lake of the Moon. At the top, the altitude is 4,577m (15,016ft), twice that of Toluca, so if you have any health problems, don't ascend (even if you are healthy, descend immediately if you feel dizzy). The view it affords of the surrounding mountains is unparalleled.

Taxco back street

7. Taxco and Cuernavaca

A two-day excursion to the silver-mining hill-town of Taxco. See map on page 42.

–Prepare for a three-hour bus ride to Taxco from the Central Autobuses del Sur terminal (beside Metro Tasquena). The route goes via Cuernavaca, a good stopover on the return leg. Cuernavaca's superb Las Mañanitas (tel: 73/14-14-66) is recommended for dinner and (if you can afford it) accommodation.–

Taxco's location on steep hills makes it a fascinating place, with ever-changing views of red-tiled roofs against green mountains, streets paved with stones laid in mosaic-like patterns, a skyline dominated by the glorious Santa Prisca church, and dozens of glinting silver shops. Taxco is the type of place that artists love to paint.

Buses of both Estrella de Oro and Flecha Roja lines have multiple daily departures from the Terminal Sur beside the Tasquena Metro station in Mexico City. The former line offers a special luxury service, showing on-board movies (dubbed into Spanish). On arrival in Taxco, you will be at the bottom of a very steep 15-minute climb up Calle de Pelita (across the street, next to the mini-super), but many white VW minivans or taxis can whisk you up quickly.

Standing facing Santa Prisca church in the small central square, the **Plaza Borda**, look up to your left to see the white sun-shades of the Hotel Agua Escondida's rooftop cafe, an excellent spot to have a drink and plan your strategy. Though most of the sights are nearby, the winding streets can be disorientating.

Santa Prisca

Santa Prisca, completed in 1758, after a decade of construction, was paid for by José de la Borda, a French silver miner who struck a particularly rich silver vein and went on to become one of the wealthiest men in Mexico. The church is considered one of the best in the country. Its carved stone facade teeming with saints and decorations is more than matched by the gilded interior, which includes paintings by Miguel Cabrera, one of the most famous artists of colonial times. Take special notice of the organ and the various gold altars.

To the right as you leave the church (still in the plaza), a plaque marks **Casa Borda**, where José de la Borda once lived. Downstairs through the adjoining arcade is the **Silver Museum**, containing work by Antonio Pineda, who in 1953 won the first of the annual contests held by local silversmiths (in particular note a chess set with pieces matching the Indians against the Conquistadors). Sr Pineda was the first apprentice of William Spratling, the Tulane University professor who arrived in Taxco in 1932 and created the local silver industry (now represented by more than 300 shops). There are no great bargains as the prices quoted are about the same as in Mexico City. The advantage here is that you can see a tremendous variety of silverwork and also watch the artisans handcraft their exquisite products.

Spratling invested much of his well-deserved riches in a collection of pre-Columbian art contained in the **William Spratling Museum**. To find the museum, walk behind the church onto Calle Veracruz (but not down the narrow steps, which becomes Mercado de Artesanías, a lively market selling almost everything).

After leaving the Spratling Museum continue walking down the hill, Calle Humboldt, and on to Ruiz de Alarcón (named for a local playwright who was a contemporary of Cervantes). Here is the **Casa de Humboldt**, where the noted German explorer/scientist Baron Alexander von Humboldt (1769–1859) stayed for a single night in 1803 during his travels in Central and South America. Vast enough to have once served as a convent and hospital and in recent years as a guesthouse owned

Artist at work

by a local architect, it now exhibits a miscellaneous collection of religious artifacts and other items. Most interesting, perhaps, are the bust and portraits of von Humboldt himself and a reproduction of a painting of a somewhat pompous-looking José de la Borda wearing a costume that must have amused even his friends.

The steep hill leading off the eastern side of Plaza Borda leads down to the shabby Plaza Bernal, at the corner of which can be found the seldom-open **Museo Grafica de la Historia Social de Taxco**, which displays early photos of the town and illustrates its evolution into the overcrowded tourist center it has become.

Taxco is one of only a few Mexican towns to have been declared a national monument, which means that residents and developers are forbidden to build in any non-local style or to change the character of the town in any way. It has understandably become a big favorite of the foreign community. A Mexican comic once drew applause by saying he had refused an invitation to visit Taxco because he didn't speak English.

Despite the considerable drawbacks of the ever-pervasive traffic, Taxco is still such an attractive town that you may want to stay overnight. There are many options ranging from clean but modest places to upmarket hotels with stunning panoramic views. (See the list of hotels in the *Practical Information* section.) Restaurants include **Cielito Lindo**, right in front of Santa Prisca, and **Sr Costillas**, upstairs on the other side of the plaza. For fine Italian dining in a romantic setting with a stunning view of the city, try the **Ventana de Taxco** in the hotel Hacienda del Solar on Highway 95 (tel: 2-05-87).

Between Taxco and Cuernavaca are two possibilities for excursions, if you have a car: **Xochicalco**, an archaeological site on a hilltop on Highway 95, is said to have been a meeting place of several Indian cultures prior to the Conquest. The **Cacahuamilpa Caves**, also on Highway 95, extend for miles but are not a good idea for claustrophobics.

Cuernavaca is not packed with tourist attractions but has some sights you may

Cathedral figurine

like to take in. The Estrella de Oro buses from Taxco arrive at the southern end of town, but you might want to walk one block north to visit the tourist office at Morelos Sur 802 before taking a taxi to the town center. The Autobuses Pullman de Morelos terminal is closer to town.

A short walk up the hill to the corner of Hidalgo will bring you to the **Cathedral de la Asunción**. Built like a fortress when Cortés had his summer home here in the 1530s, it is rather plain except

Palacio de Cortés

for some curious frescoes depicting the persecution of Christian missionaries in Japan. A rare statue believed to be of Cortés sits at the entrance. At one time the Franciscans had a monastery here and the skull and crossbones above the portico is the symbol of their Order. The **Museo Casa Robert Brady** has a fascinating collection of Mexican art and Asian handicrafts but it is open for only a few hours a day Thursday to Saturday.

On the western side of the cathedral, you'll find an interesting group of paintings depicting Indians at work in pre-colonial days in the **Palacio Municipal**, to which admission is free on weekday mornings and afternoons (but not between noon and 2pm).

Walk across the street to have a soda and study the informative paintings about Emperor Maximilian and Carlotta in the cafe at the entrance to the **Jardín Borda**. The Borda gardens, which once surrounded the 18th-century home of Taxco's richest silver magnate, were restored a few years ago and are exceptionally pleasant with fountains, lake and outdoor theater.

Coming out of the Jardín Borda, turn left along Hidalgo and past the post office to the **Jardín Jurez** (designed by Gustav Eiffel). Adjoining is the larger **Jardín de los Heroes,** or Alameda, at the eastern end of which is the **Palacio de Cortés**, which Cortés built as a summer home on the ruins of an old Indian temple. Now a museum, with a strong colonial flavour, it boasts a mural by Diego Rivera depicting almost 400 years of Mexican history with all its famous heroes and villains. For more than half a century before the 'Where's Wally?' concept caught on, it has been challenging Mexican children to identify the participants in their national saga.

Because of its temperate climate Cuernavaca been been the prime resort for *capitalinos* since Aztec times but has never had much to

Rivera mural

offer tourists except for excellent hotels. One is **Las Mañanitas**, on Calle Ricardo Linares, six blocks north of the city center. If you've ever dreamed of staying in a flower-filled garden in which fountains tinkle and peacocks strut, sleeping in a room with period furniture and eating first-rate food, now is the time.

At Casa Robert Brady

Shopping

The major shopping area of Mexico City, certainly as far as tourists are concerned, is not downtown but the Zona Rosa, a patchwork of streets with European names off the Paseo de la Reforma about 2km (1 mile) from the Alameda. It is not a very large area (it extends approximately from Niza to Florencia and from Reforma to Insurgentes), so you should be able to cover the entire area quite easily on foot.

Start at **Sanborns** at the corner of Niza and Hamburgo, checking out their extensive offerings of silver jewelry, picture frames and the like. Continue straight ahead on Hamburgo on the right side to **Miniaturas** where you can see a complete array of Lilliputian objects; **Amarras** next door specializes in casual clothes with a nautical motif; at the corner of Copenhague visit **Gaitán**, a long-time landmark in the Zona for ranch-style leather goods. Just ahead at the corner of Genova is **Zaga**, a Zona Rosa menswear institution since the 1960s.

Turn right on Genova for the **Librairie Française**. Besides books and periodicals in French, check out their graphics. Looping back down Genova, going past McDonald's to the corner, you'll notice gaily-colored talavera ware at the corner of Londres at **Escalera**; check out the shop next door around the corner on Londres for decorative Mexican pieces with a touch of the fine arts. **El Buho Soñador** is next, with cocktail dresses and sweaters by young designers; **Artesanías Finas Patricia**, is known for well-made embroidered clothes. **Yo** across the street has handknit cotton sweaters and upstairs a few steps away is a small **Fonart** store, always good for arts and crafts.

Mexican motifs

Further along Reforma, to the east of Chapultepec Park, is the upscale district, Polanco. The **museum shop** of the Centro Cultural de Arte Contemporaneo, on Campos Eliseos, stocks items inspired by past exhibits. Back outside, cross over to **Cesar Franco** for quality knitwear and then turn right on to Galileo to visit the **Pyrelongue** store for expensive watches.

60

Good for gifts: the Centro Cultural de Arte Contemporaneo

Cross the street at Emilio Castelar to see a whole series of restaurants (*tacos*, crêpes, pita bread, chicken). Continue along Polanco park and turn right at Alejandro Dumás to take in the many specialty shops catering to local residents. This is the place to buy newspapers from all around the world, maids' uniforms complete with aprons, and a stunning array of beautiful plants. **Cherchez la Femme** at Julio Verne 95 specializes in sensational house-designed and imported haute couture buttons.

Plaza Polanco, at Oscar Wilde and Presidente Mazaryk, offers shops, restaurants and people-watching in a 1940s California-inspired building. Presidente Mazaryk has around a dozen small shopping centers and international brand-name stores stretching all the way down to Mariano Escobedo. The smaller outlets are always changing, so stroll along to see what's new and in style. If you'd like to visit a larger Mexican mall nearby, go to **Pabellón Polanco** at Ejercito Nacional and Váquez de Melia. The fast-food section offers traditional favorites as well as international cuisine. It is often full of local students and executives at lunchtime.

Markets

The capital's numerous *mercados* are always lively, invariably offering bigger bargains than the regular stores. All are open daily, including Sunday. One word of caution, however: markets are not for everyone — what for some is a fascinating slice of life is for others an overwhelming assault on the senses and sensibilities.

The biggest is probably the immense **Merced** (at the Merced Metro station), a huge place with as much going on outside as there is under cover. Sounds and smells are almost overpowering: chickens frying, radios blaring and

Bags and baskets

Sonora Market

men with loudspeakers; ice-filled buckets of fish; girls rolling, heating and filling *tortillas* from an array of plastic bowls; old men bent double with the weight of sacks of potatoes or beans.

A few blocks away, on Fray Servando Teresa de Mier at Rosari, is the **Sonora Market** specializing in witchcraft items, herbs and live animals, where the sacred rubs shoulders with the pagan. The atmosphere here is subdued, almost reverent. At one end is the animal market, where ducks, turkeys, rabbits, doves, parrots, puppies, canaries and exotic animals can all be bought.

Almost as large as the Merced is the **Lagunilla Market**, three blocks along Rayón, about three blocks north of the Plaza Garibaldi. The main street divides it into two sections: the area to the north is the most intriguing, filled with clouds of aromatic steam and men with knives, choppers and hatchets slashing, cutting and scraping countless pineapples, cactus leaves, carrots and slabs of meat and fish. The other market is mostly devoted to clothes, its

Art for sale

narrow aisles lined with embroidered *charro* hats, children's party dresses and mannequins draped with sequinned party clothes.

The **San Juan Market** (on Ayuntamiento at Dolores; walk three blocks south on the Eje Central Lázaro Cárdenas and turn right) boasts 176 stores selling handicrafts, souvenirs, etc. A few blocks further east along Ayuntamiento at Balderas is the more interesting **Artesanías de la Ciudadela**, a less formal market with a much wider range of Mexican crafts. If you need to establish some prices to back up your bargaining, first visit the fixed-price government craft store opposite the Juarez monument on the Alameda.

Saturdays only

Bazar Sábado and park art show in San Angel offers a flavor of past Mexico and is a good place to buy beautiful or amusing handicrafts. Alternatively visit the flea market in Plaza del Angel in the Zona Rosa, which offers fun browsing in a compact shopping center devoted to antiques. Get there around 11am–1pm, when it's most lively.

Eating Out

It's hard to find dull food in Mexico City: even very modest places offer tasty food for a modest price. Authentic Mexican cooking comprises a range of regional cuisines and a combination of Spanish and Indian ingredients. The Europeans contributed beef, pork, lamb, chicken, rice and oranges and the locals many varieties of chile, tomato, turkey, corn, chocolate and peanuts.

With thousands of restaurants in the capital, most nations are represented and so-called international cuisine is widely available. Argentinian-style steakhouses are popular (try the *chimichurri* sauce) as are Italian restaurants and there are more and more Oriental restaurants, with Río Tiber street, which begins at the Angel monument, now almost a Japanese town, as far as eating goes (*sushi* is big here). Pizzas, hamburgers and *tacos* are everywhere. Don't miss *tacos al carbón,* thin beefsteaks charcoaled before your very eyes, then chopped up for do-it-yourself *tacos* in soft, warm *tortillas* and served with a choice of delicious sauces.

Locals careful of their health do not eat at the eateries you find on the sidewalk, and it's sensible to follow their example. There are hundreds of options for memorable dining, even when you're in a hurry. Remember that lunch is late in Mexico, starting at 2pm, so take that into consideration if you want a fine meal, as the *platos del día* will probably not be ready till then. In the following list, $ = under $10 (per person, including one drink); $$ = $10–25; $$$ over $25.

Alfresco dining at Hotel Majestic

Downtown

CAFÉ DE TACUBA
Tacuba 28
Tel: 518-49-50
With its vaulted ceilings, tiled wainscoting, large paintings and humorous mural in the back. Go for the atmosphere. $$

CASINO ESPAÑOL
Isabel la Católica 34
Tel: 521–88-94
Spanish food in a splendidly ornate interior. $$

HOTEL DE CORTÉS
Hidalgo 85
Tel: 518-21-81
Offers open-air patio delightful for lunch or drinks. $$

LA TERRAZA
7th floor, Hotel Majestic
Madero 73
Tel: 521-86-00
Alfresco dining under parasols, overlooking the most important plaza in the nation. $$

L'HERITAGE
5 de Mayo 10-A
Tel: 512-73-60
Where businessmen, bankers and politicians meet for power breakfasts. Cozy and dignified. $$

Dine under murals at Prendes

EL REY DE PAVO
Palma, between Madero and 16 de Septiembre
Traditional turkey dishes; offers an extensive menu. $$

PRENDES
16 de Septiembre 10-C
Tel: 521-54-04
Dine beside murals packed with portraits of famous patrons. Prendes has been a favorite for 100 years. Note: lunch only, with service from 1.30–5.30pm. $$

SANBORNS CASA DE LOS AZULEJOS
Madero and Condesa
Tel: 518-10-26
This famous establishment remains a firm favorite that features a dramatic patio. $$

Sanborns' Casa de los Azulejos

Zona Rosa area

BEATRIZ
Londres 179
Tel: 525-58-57
Economical *tacos* and soups at a perennially popular spot. $

BELLINGHAUSEN
Londres 179
Tel: 207-40-49
German specialties, popular with businessmen. Old-fashioned ambience and attentive service. $$$

BELLINI
Reforma 373 (near Angel monument)
Tel: 207-89-44
Very upscale Italian, with excellent service. $$$

CHALET SUIZO
Niza 37
Tel: 208-74-32
Swiss chalet setting (knotted pine and check tablecloths) and hearty food. $$

FONDA EL REFUGIO
Liverpool 166
Tel: 207-27-32
Country-elegant, an institution for excellent Mexican cuisine. $$$

LA MANSION
Hamburgo 77
Tel: 514-32-47
One of a chain of restaurants serving excellent Argentinian-style steaks. $$

LUAU
Niza 38
Tel: 525-74-74
Cantonese Chinese with elegant low lighting. $$

RAFFAELLO
Londres 165
Tel: 525-65-85
Post-modern chalet serving Italian food. $$

PARIS 16
Reforma 368
Almost at the corner of Varsovia
Tel: 511-01-19
A yuppie hangout with an ever-changing collection of paintings for sale. Popular for lunch. (Not visible from street.) $$

YUG
Varsovia 3
Tel: 533-32-96
Vegetarian restaurant with a lunch buffet. A favorite with the local office workers. $

Piled high in Polanco

Polanco

BENKAY
Hotel Nikko, Campos Eliseos 204
Tel: 280-00-15
Haute Japanese cuisine. $$$

CHEZ WOK
Tennyson 117, corner Presidente Mazarik
Tel: 282-10-42
Old pictures and imperial Chinese cuisine. Posh clientele. $$$

CREPAS VINCY
Emilio Castelar
Small spot for a fast meal – high-tech decor in French flag colors. $$

HACIENDA DE LOS MORALES
Vázquez de Mella 525
Tel: 540-32-25

Several dining rooms in stately former *hacienda* – part of Polanco was
carved out of its land. $$

LAGO CHAPULTEPEC
Segunda Sección Chapultepec
Lago Mayor
Tel: 515-95-85
For very elegant dining and dancing
in striking modern setting with enor-
mous windows overlooking fountain
and lake, with Polanco skyline in dis-
tance. You'll need to take a taxi or
drive, as it's in the new section of the
park. $$$

LA PETITE FRANCE
Presidente Mazarik 360
Tel: 550-01-41
Greenhouse setting, serving French
food. Popular with powerlunchers. $$

LAS MERCEDES
Darwin 113, corner Leibnitz
Tel: 254-50-00
Fine Mexican food and a welcoming
ambience. Advisable to make reserva-
tions if you don't want to stand in
line. $$

A bottle stall

LOS ALMENDRIS
Campos Eliseos 164
Tel: 203-46-43
Mexico City branch of famous Yucatán
restaurants specializing in regional Yu-
catán dishes. $$

MAXIM'S
Hotel Presidente, Campos Eliseos 218
Tel: 281-02-49
Art Nouveau splendor and French cui-
sine in the Mexican branch of the fa-
mous Parisian establishment. $$$

SIR WINSTON CHURCHILL'S
Blvd Avila Camacho 67
On the Periférico
Tel: 520-05-85
Tudor house with a warm but formal
ambience. Serves great roast beef. $$$

SPAGLIA
Hómero 704
Tel: 203-03-06
Lunch with trendy, yuppie crowd. $$

TUTTO BENE
Pabellón Polanco (mall)
Hómero and Vázquez de Mella
Tel: 395-79-42
Modern Mediterranean setting for re-
gional dishes from all over Italy. $$

Insurgentes heading south

BENIHANA
Insurgentes Sur 640
Tel: 523–33-85
Famous Japanese steakhouse. $$

EL NUEVO CAFÉ DE PARIS
Vito Alessio Robles 82
Tel: 661-06-63
French food in airy, black and white
interior. $$

GRUTA EHDEN
Pino 69
Tel: 661-19-94
The best Lebanese food since 1930 at
a location off the tourist track. $$

LA MANSION
Insurgentes Sur 778
Tel: 523-20-00
The original Argentinian steakhouse.
Try the *chimichurri* sauce. $$

L'ITALIANO
Insurgentes Sur 729
Tel: 523-33-46
Popular, upmarket Italian. $$$

MAZURKA
Nueva York 150
Tel: 523-88-11
Polish food, in former private home. $$$

SUNTORY
Torres de Adalid 14
Tel: 669-46-76
Fine Japanese cuisine in stately dining rooms. $$$

LA PERGOLA
Insurgentes
Tel: 395-26-92
Lots of pictures, dark interior, Italian cuisine. $$

San Angel

CARLOS 'N CHARLIE'S
Altavista 67
Tel: 616-16-73
Enjoy traditional tasty food in a fun atmosphere, presided over by a mural of baby angels. $$

DOS PUERTAS
Pedro Luis Ogazón 102
Half a block from Insurgentes,
San Angel
Tel: 661-42-88
Very attractive, sophisticated-rustic setting. $$

LA CAVA
Insurgentes Sur
Tel: 616-13-76
Mexican modern decor, delicious food. $$

LANCER'S STEAKHOUSE
Insurgentes Sur
Tel: 661-56-65
Some of the best steaks in town. $$

LOS IRABIEN
Av de la Paz
Tel: 660-23-82
Elegant and cozy, with original paintings on the walls. $$$

Los Irabien, San Angel

SAN ANGEL INN
Calle Palma 50
Tel: 548-67-46
This establishment is one of the most beautiful restaurants in Mexico City. Strolling musicians play romantic music at tables. $$

Coyoacán

EL TAJIN
Av M A de Quevedo 687
(Centro Veracruzano)
Tel: 659-44-47
Nouvelle Mexican cuisine by renowned gourmet chef Alicia Gironella De'Angeli. Lunch only. $$

Restaurant Chains

While not offering *haute cuisine*, Mexican chains offer tasty food, fast service, a pleasant atmosphere and are consistently clean, with the added advantage of having outlets all over the city and beyond. Popular chains include **California**, **Sanborns**, **Toks** and **VIPS**. **La Parrilla Suiza** is a chain devoted to *tacos al carbón* (charcoal grilled meat) and melted cheese served in tiny earthenware bowls. It is a favorite with locals.

Nightlife

Mexico City offers an array of options for evening entertainment, from elegant dining at a posh restaurant to watching a fast *jai alai* game, dancing the night away at a discotheque, attending a classical music concert or enjoying free performances by *mariachi* groups in Plaza Garibaldi. Most office workdays end at 7pm at the earliest, so things get going rather late. Major international performers include Mexico City on their schedules: check *The News*, an English-language newspaper, for what's current or, if you read Spanish, buy the weekly magazine *Tiempo Libre*, which lists movies, dance performances, restaurants, TV, theater, etc. Tickets for all kinds of events can be bought from **Ticketmaster** at Mixup, a music store at Genova 74, in the Zona Rosa (tel: 325-90-00) where you can also obtain a brochure listing upcoming events.

Bars

All hotels have bars. Two of the most popular with locals are **Stouffer Presidente**, Campos Eliseos 218, in Polanco, where entertainment in the lobby bar alternates between live chamber music and jazz, and **María Isabel Sheraton**, the place to go for quiet conversation. **La Opera**, Av 5 de Mayo 10, has an authentic turn-of-the-century cantina. **Bellim**, World Trade Center, Insurgentes Ave., offers a magnificent view of the city from 37 floors up.

Dance Performances

The **Ballet Folklórico** presents a range of Mexican dances at polished performances on Wednesday and Sunday evenings at the Palacio de Bellas Artes, Eje Central Lázaro Cárdenas, at the eastern end of the Alameda. Tickets can be purchased at the box office (you will have to go in person to reserve seats in advance).

Another, newer Mexican dance company which is worth seeing is the **Ballet Folklórico Nacional Aztlán**. It performs at the refurbished historic Teatro de la Ciudad, Donceles 36 (tel: 510-21-97).

To see flamenco dancers in *de rigueur* nightclub settings you should visit **Gitanerías**, Oaxaca, right by the Insurgentes Metro station traffic circle (tel: 208-22-64), or **El Corral de la Morería**, Londres 161, Zona Rosa (tel: 525-17-62), whose doors open at 10pm (the show itself doesn't begin until around midnight, when things start to hot up).

Discos and Nightclubs

Your best bet is to try **Cero Cero**, Hotel Camino Real, Leibnitz 100 (tel: 203-21-21); open 9pm–4am. This nightclub attracts an upscale clientele and it is necessary to make reservations on weekends when it is especially packed. **The Centro Historico** is full of all kinds of nightspots. Check *Tiempo Libre* for listings.

Try **El Patio**, Atenas 9 (tel: 535-39-04), 9pm–4am, for dinner and dancing. **Las Sillas,** Hotel Crowne Plaza, Reforma 80 (tel: 705-15-15), provides live music every evening except Sundays.

Jai Alai

If you fancy a Mexican sports evening, among a betting public, consider attending a *jai alai* game. In this very fast sport the ball is thrust against a wall using a basket scoop (in a manner similar to squash). Games usually begin at 7.30pm at **Frontón México**, Plaza de la República No 17, by the Monumento a la Revolución, but there may be a strike that stops play. Men are required to wear a jacket and tie. A bilingual brochure explains the betting system.

Movies

Many theaters show US movies a few months after they are released in the United States. The English-language daily *The News* has weekly movie listings. Spanish-language papers publish lists daily, with the titles translated into Spanish. *Tiempo Libre* offers the most complete listing (look under *cine*). Performances are at set times, and subtitles are used rather than dubbing except in the case of animated and children's films.

Music

Classical Music and Opera: Venues include **Palacio de Bellas Artes**, Eje Central Lázaro Cárdenas (tel: 709-31-11) and **Sala Netzahualcoyotl**, Centro Cultural Universitario, Insurgentes Sur 3000. The Sala Netzahualcoyotl offers great acoustics but it is possibly too far off the beaten track unless you have local friends with a car who can give you a lift.

Jazz: Try the **Lobby bar of the Hotel Galería Plaza**, Hamburgo 195, in the Zona Rosa, or **New Orleans**, Avenida Revolución, San Angel (tel: 550-19-08) for what is considered by the locals to be 'classic' jazz. Or you

Palacio de Bellas Artes, venue for classical music

could try **La Casona del Elefante**, Plaza San Jacinto 9, San Angel, located next to the Bazar del Sábado, offers mellow jazz on Friday and Saturday evenings.

Latin American Rhythms: Antillano's, Francisco Pimentel 74, Colonia San Rafael (tel: 592-04-39), offers hip-wiggling salsa, etc, from 9pm. For great atmosphere try **Bar León**, Brasil No 5, near the Zócalo, Wednesdays to Saturdays, but go in a group for safety, as this bar is out of the main tourist area.

Mariachis: the heart-breaking songs of the *mariachi* bands can be enjoyed for free in **Plaza Garibaldi**, Eje Central Lázaro Cárdenas. Wander round listening to different groups competing for business, then have a drink at **Tlaquepaque** or **Tenampa**. **La Mancha** in the Hotel Aristos, Zona Rosa, Reforma 276, is a good option if you want to enjoy *mariachis* in more luxurious surroundings.

Peñas: These are coffee-houses-cum-bars where you will find the kind of South American music that Simon and Garfunkel copied and popularized in *El Condor Pasa* – bamboo flutes, *jarangos* (a small stringed instrument), guitars, voices. Try **El Mesón de la Guitarra**, Félix Cuevas 332, in the vicinity of Liverpool department store (tel: 559-15-35). Another possibility worth trying is **El Condor Pasa**, Rafael Checa No 1, San Angel, near El Carmen church.

Rock: Hard Rock Café, Campos Eliseos 291 (tel: 327-71-00). If you fancy something familiar the Mexican outlet of the famous international chain has a restaurant, bar and disco. **Rockotitlán**, Insurgentes Sur 952 (tel: 687-78-93), offers live music in an intimate atmosphere.

Trio Music: El Jorongo Bar, Hotel María Isabel Sheraton, Paseo de la Reforma 325.

Veracruz Music, with harp, guitars and lively singing, can be heard at **La Fonda del Recuerdo**, Bahía de las Palmas 39-A.

People-watching

This popular pastime is best enjoyed in the **Zona Rosa** or the plazas of **Coyoacán**. Stroll around and then settle down at a cafe for a drink and supper. For a pricey dinner worth saving for, go to **Copenhague Street** in the Zona Rosa and choose between the many restaurants with outdoor or indoor tables.

Variety Shows

Teatro Blanquita, Plaza Serdán 16 on the Eje Central Lázaro Cárdenas, across from Plaza Garibaldi, is the biggest and best-known in the city, with comic acts interspersed with pop music. Although performances are in Spanish, the acts are so varied that language is only a minor handicap. Before or after the performance here, it's a good idea to visit Plaza Garibaldi (almost across the street), where you can listen to impromptu performances by the *mariachi* bands (see opposite). Teatro Blanquita is open Thursday to Saturday 7–9.30pm and Sunday 6–8.30pm.

A mariachi band

Calendar of Special Events

Most of Mexico's hundreds of fiestas are religious in basis but combine Indian elements with Spanish and Catholic characteristics, including fireworks, processions, dancing and feasting. Wonderful occasions for letting off steam, they are celebrated with great intensity. Everyone has not only a birthday but a saint's day as well, so each individual has two personal feast days. Some of the most important annual events in Mexico City are listed here. You should also look out for special sporting events.

January – March

6 January: **Día de los Reyes**, celebrated with special wreath-shaped cakes with dolls of Jesus hidden inside. Anyone whose slice contains a doll must give a party of *tamales* and *atole* on February 2. Children receive toys on this day instead of Christmas.

17 January: **Feast of San Antonio Abad** – blessing of animals at parish churches.

5 February: **Constitution Day**.

24 February: **Día de la Bandera** (Flag Day) is celebrated largely by school-children with processions of the national flag. A special song is sung for the occasion.

Holy Week (in March or April). Passion play in Ixtapalapa neighborhood in Mexico City includes a mock Crucifixion on **Good Friday** and in Taxco there is a candlelit procession. On **Holy Saturday**, papiermâché figures of Judas are burned.

April – June

Festival del Centro Histórico, an annual cultural event, at a variable date in April, with concerts, exhibitions and gourmet meals held at various venues. Celebrations last for two weeks.

25 April: **Celebration of San Marcos** in Axcapotzalco and Milpa Alta.

1 May: **Labor Day** parade.

3 May: **Día de la Santa Cruz** (Feast of the Holy Cross). Construction workers place crosses festooned with paper decorations on the buildings they're working on. Churches hold processions.

10 May: **Mother's Day**. Mothers get half a day off in most offices, and restaurants are filled with celebrating families.

Bullfighting: a perennial celebration of daring and grace

June: **Nopal fair** (edible cactus), Milpa Alta.

June: **Corpus Christi**. Street vendors sell straw mules symbolizing the one Christ rode, and churches have processions.

July – September

10 July–1 August: **Feria Metropolitana del Libro** (Metropolitan Book Fair).

Festival Latino Canolfilo (dog show). Exact date varies.

15 September: **El Grito** ceremony in Zócalo. At 11pm the president re-enacts an event of Mexican Independence by appearing on the balcony of the National Palace and shouting ¡Viva México! among other invocations, which are echoed by the crowd. There is a firework display and a military parade is held the following day.

October – December

Cervantino Festival. Although based in the city of Guanajuato, this cultural feast attracts artistic performers from around the world, including dance troupes, symphony orchestras, classical soloists, etc. A number of cultural events are scheduled in the capital.

1 November: The president gives his *Informe Anual*, a very long speech on the state of the country.

1–2 November: **Día de los Muertos** (Day of the Dead). People take food and drink into the cemeteries for their dear departed (*muertitos*). Especially colorful at Ajijíc.

November: **International Film Festival** – a two-week event staged in theaters throughout the city.

12 December: **Feast of the Virgin of Guadalupe**. Pilgrimages to the Basilica to honor the patron saint.

16–24 December: Every year special parties, *posadas*, are held to commemorate Mary and Joseph's search for an inn in Bethlehem. In private homes all participants carry candles and at one point half of them go outside to request a room in song while the other half remain indoors, playing the part of the innkeepers.

Nativity plays called *Pastorelas* are staged at different points in the city. They can be occasions of great hilarity. One of the best is held at the church in Tepotzotlán, just north of Mexico City.

PRACTICAL information

GETTING THERE

By Air

The Benito Juárez International Airport in Mexico City is served by most major international airlines. The US carriers offer direct service to Mexico City with connecting flights to other destinations (Acapulco and Guadalajara) and include American, Alaska, America West, Continental, Delta and Northwest. From Canada choose between Air Canada and Canadian Airlines International. From Europe you can fly with Aeroflot, Air France, Alitalia, British Airways, Iberia, KLM, Lufthansa and Swissair. The national airlines of Israel, Japan and Singapore also fly to Mexico City. The largest Mexican airlines are Aeroméxico, Mexicana and Taesa, all of which offer national and international services. Check with your travel agent for discount tickets.

For reliable ground transport upon arrival, go to the booths selling fixed price taxi tickets, located just beside the arrival lounges. After stating your destination, you will be given a ticket and charged according to the zone. There are no airport buses and although the subway has a stop beside the domestic terminal, you are not permitted to take more than one small bag aboard.

By Rail

Mexico has an extensive rail network operated by the government-owned Ferrocarriles Nacionales de México. The disadvantage of coming to Mexico City from either Central America or the US is that you cannot reserve in advance and must take a chance on getting a seat, once you have crossed the border. It is also possible to go by bus to Monterrey and take the daily Regiomontano train, which leaves at 6pm and arrives at 9am. With a *camarín* or *alcoba* (single or double pullman) ticket, you can have a leisurely supper, a drink in the club car and retire for a comfortable night's sleep. In general, however, your best bet is to fly into the city and use the railroad for travel within the country.

By Road

There are many independent buslines providing services just about everywhere in the country and several classes of service are available, including luxury coaches offering reclining seats, on-board movies, air conditioning and refreshments. The closest US border point is Laredo, Texas, and

Taxis are cheap and plentiful

Raising the flag over the Zócalo

the trip takes at least 12 hours. So if your stay is limited, fly in and take the bus to places you want to visit.

Driving to Mexico is an attractive option for US residents. You will need a special permit, proof of ownership of the car such as the vehicle registration, and possibly a credit card. The requirements for bringing a car into the country often change, so check with the AAA and/or the nearest Mexican consulate for the current requirements. Although your regular driver's license is valid in Mexico, it's a good idea to get local insurance, as foreign policies do not provide coverage.

Mexico City's *Hoy No Circula* (Day Without a Car) program prohibits the use of your car one day per week. The last number of your license plate determines which day: 5 and 6 Monday; 7 and 8 Tuesday; 3 and 4 Wednesday; 1 and 2 Thursday; 9, 0 and custom plates Friday.

TRAVEL ESSENTIALS

When to Visit / Weather

Any time of the year is good but the rainy season, from May to October, means that there is a downpour at some point every day, although it is generally sunny before and after. It seldom rains between November and May, but there is sometimes a lot of dust in the air. February is called *Febrero loco* because several types of weather can occur in the same day. When visiting spots such as Cuernavaca, only 45 minutes away but several thousand feet lower in altitude, you will feel more comfortable in light summer cottons than the lightweight wool clothing needed in Mexico City. Put on a sweater over your 'Cuernavaca clothes' and shed it upon arrival.

Visas

People from most countries will need a valid passport with visa, smallpox vaccination and a tourist card to enter Mexico. Canadian and US citizens need only a tourist card or FMT (obtained at the airport) upon presenting proof of citizenship (birth certificate, passport, voter's registration or military ID). These are valid for 30, 60, 90 or 180 days. It's wise to ask for more time than you think you'll need to avoid the red tape involved in obtaining an extension.

Clothing

Due to its 2,286m (7,500ft) elevation above sea-level, Mexico City is cool at nights and a sweater or jacket is required year round in the evening. Temperatures sometimes fall to freezing in winter. If you're planning an extended stay, note that few hotels or houses have central heating, so you sometimes have to wear warmer clothing indoors than out. It's a good idea to dress in layers that can be removed as the day progresses and temperatures rise and replaced in the late afternoon and evening as it gets cool again. Spring and early summer have been quite warm in recent years, making cotton or linen the most comfortable fabrics. The usual style of dress is quite formal, and slacks are therefore more in keeping with local customs than shorts. Some restaurants won't let men in without ties, so be sure to bring one along. As you ascend or descend in altitude on excursions outside the city, you'll need slightly warmer clothing (for Toluca) or warm weather wear (for Cuernavaca and Taxco).

Electricity

110 volts, 60-cycle alternating current as in the US. There are sometimes outages or fluctuations.

Time Zone

Mexico City is on US Central Standard Time.

GETTING ACQUAINTED

Geography and Population

Situated on the central plateau in the Valley of Mexico, the capital is surrounded by majestic mountain peaks, part of the Sierra Nevada mountain range, with the snow-capped volcanoes Popocatépetl and Ixtaccíhuatl, the second and third highest peaks in the country, sometimes visible. The valley floor was once the site of huge lakes, which have either dried up or been drained over the centuries. The drainage projects were carried out to eliminate the disastrous floods that had previously plagued the capital.

The population of the Mexico City metropolitan area is over 20 million and still growing. The urban area now sprawls into the neighboring states. The principal religion is Roman Catholicism, mixed with a liberal smattering of pre-Hispanic rituals and beliefs.

MONEY MATTERS

The Mexican currency presently in use is the *peso*, indicated by $. The New Peso marking was dropped in 1994 shortly after it was introduced in 1993 to get rid of three zeros from the bills – the computers couldn't handle the big numbers.

Only the new currency is in circulation. The *peso* bills are in denomination of 10, 20, 50, 100, 200 and 500, while coins are now 1, 2, 5, 10 and 20 *pesos* and 5, 10, 20, and 50 *centavos*.

The *peso* coins have a contrasting colored metal border, while the *centavos* are small silver or copper-colored pieces, some so thin and tiny (the 5 and 10 *centavos* coins) that they are hard to pick up.

Old *peso* coins and bills are no longer legal tender, though you may be passed them 'by mistake'.

To simplify the conversion of prices into US dollars, you can ask for a conversion card. They are available in hotels and travel agencies.

Foreign currency can be changed at the many exchange houses called *Casa de Cambio*. Rates vary from one to the other, so if you are in an area where there are several (such as downtown, Reforma or the Zona Rosa), compare the rates. Major credit cards are accepted.

GETTING AROUND

Subway

The extensive subway system (now nine lines and still growing) is inexpensive to use ($1.30 a ticket) and can quickly take you to many places in the city, without you running the risk of getting lost that you have to take on a bus. Maps are available at the information booths in major stations. Mexicans are justly proud of their Metro, which is clean and has attractive stations with marble floors. Some stations

The Church: an abiding influence

are decorated with murals and architectural models or show art exhibits. During morning and evening rush hours, some stations will board only women and children in the end cars to protect them from the crush.

Taxis and Buses

Taxis are quite reasonably priced compared with their counterparts in many other world capitals. Make sure that the meter is running and starts at $3 for yellow cabs and $3,60 for green. After 11pm the charge rises to the meter reading plus 20 percent. Taxi drivers wanting to take advantage of tourists, especially in hotel zones, sometimes attempt to charge a flat fee that is several times the normal price. There are special taxis parked outside hotels with English-speaking drivers, who will take you on tours around the city as well as to the most popular tourist destinations. They generally drive large sedans and are much more expensive than those cruising on the street, but you may feel more comfortable and secure using this means of transport.

For hire

Car Rentals

Although not everyone feels up to tackling Mexico City traffic, there is a wide variety of rental options for those who do. Prices range from around US$60–70 per day for the smallest model car, with insurance. Some of the many agencies are: Budget (Tel: 566-68-00); Hertz (Tel: 281-38-25) and Grey Line Rent a Car (Tel: 208-11-63; fax: 208-28-38). Telephone numbers seem to change frequently, so it's best to consult the *Sección Amarilla* (Yellow Pages) of the phone book, looking under '*automoviles – renta de.*'

HOURS AND HOLIDAYS
Business Hours

Banks keep odd hours: some are open 8am–7pm while others keep to the more traditional 9am–3pm hours. Stores are open 10am–7pm during the week, 10am–8pm on Saturdays and many are now open on Sundays. Office hours for most businesses are 9am–6 or 7pm, with a lengthy break for lunch (usually 1–4pm).

Public Holidays

Banks, government offices, schools and stores are generally closed on the following dates:

January 1	**New Year's Day**
February 5	**Constitution Day**
March 21	**Birthday of Benito Juárez**
March/April	**Holy Week: Holy Thursday and Good Friday**
May 1	**Labor Day**
September 16	**Independence Day**
November 2	**Day of the Dead**
November 20	**Revolution Day**
December 25	**Christmas Day**

ACCOMMODATION

Mexico City is well provided with hotels at all price levels. Space does not permit an inclusive listing, but the selection that follows has something for everyone. For a more complete view of what's available, consult your travel agent. Hotels in some of the nearby cities are also included. In the following list $$$ = $100 dollars per night (per double room); $$ = $50–100; $ = under $50.

Downtown

CASA DE LOS AMIGOS
Ignacio Mariscal 132
Tel: 705-06-46
Budget accommodation in Quaker-run guesthouse. Clean and well-located with the latest guidebooks available for serious travelers. $

HOTEL MAJESTIC
Av Madero 73
Tel: 521-86-00
A good option if you want an unforgettable view on to the Zócalo and colonial decor. Cautions: rooms on Madero may be very noisy and those facing interior court afford little privacy. $$

HOTEL RITZ
Av Madero 30
Tel: 518-13-40, Fax: 518-3466
Gloomy, older-style hotel but convenient for those wanting downtown location. US television channels. $$

HOTEL DE CORTÉS
Av Hidalgo 85, behind the Alameda
Tel: 518-21-82
Charming and old-fashioned hotel, conveniently situated. $$

HOTEL FIESTA PALACE
Paseo de la Reforma 80
Tel: 566-77-77
Large, efficient hotel on Glorieta de Colón. Business center. $$$

Hotel Calinda Geneve

Zona Rosa area

HOTEL CALINDA GENEVE
Londres 130
Tel: 211-00-71
Refurbished old hotel, now contains Sanborns. $$

HOTEL MARIA CRISTINA
Río Lerma 31
Tel: 535-99-50
A refurbished old hotel with nostalgic atmosphere. $$

HOTEL MARCO POLO
Amberes 27
Tel: 207-18-93
Small establishment with all amenities. $$$

HOTEL MARIA ISABEL SHERATON
Paseo de la Reforma 325
Tel: 207-39-33
Excellent location for both business travelers and tourists, at Angel Monument. Large and luxurious, with all facilities, including a business center. $$$

HOTEL WESTIN GALERIA PLAZA
Hamburgo 195
Tel: 211-00-14
Fashionable location in the middle of the Zona Rosa. $$$

Puebla

HOTEL DEL PORTAL
M Avila Camacho y Portal Morelos
Tel: (22) 46-02-11
Convenient location right on the Zócalo. Satellite TV. $$

MESON DEL ANGEL
Hermanos Serdán 807
Tel: (22) 24-30-00
Three buildings offering a choice of colonial or modern architecture, plus two swimming pools, tennis courts, restaurants and bars. Near the Puebla exit on toll road from Mexico City, about 6km (4 miles) from downtown. $$

Taxco

HOTEL POSADA DE LA MISION
John F Kennedy 32
Tel: (762) 2-00-63
A rustic stone building (formerly the old Spanish mission) on the hilltop facing the church of Santa Prisca, offering spectacular views from rooms and a restaurant. $$

HOTEL SANTA PRISCA
Cena Oscura 1
Tel: (762) 2-0080
Only a block from the plaza, this older establishment is right in the heart of things. Has plenty of charm and is reasonably priced $$

Toluca

HOTEL COLONIAL
Hidalgo Oriente 103
Tel: (72) 15-97-00
Colonial, faded grandeur atmosphere in convenient downtown location. $

HOTEL DEL REY
Carretera México-Toluca Km. 63.5
Tel: (72) 17-96-02
This comfortable, modern hotel is located on the industrial strip leading into town. $$

Querétaro

MESON SANTA ROSA
Pasteur 17
Tel: (42) 14-5781
A beautiful and charming hotel. $$

HEALTH AND EMERGENCIES

Medical Services

If you should take sick on your trip and need immediate attention, the first thing to do is call the front desk of your hotel and ask for the hotel doctor, who will provide fast service and in the best hotels probably speak English. In less urgent cases many hotels will be able to provide a list of English-speaking doctors and dentists in the area.

In the case of a non-English-speaking guest needing medical assistance, hotel staff will help contact the embassy of the person concerned, which will have its own list of doctors. Two hospitals preferred by foreigners and well-off Mexicans are:

HOSPITAL ABC, The American British Cowdray Hospital, Sur 136 (corner Av Observatorio), Col Las Américas, tel: 272-85-00.

HOSPITAL ANGELES DEL PEDREGAL, Camino Santa Teresa 1055, Col Héroes de Padierna, tel: 652-11-88.

For medicines, most Sanborns have a pharmacy section and there are *Farmacias* throughout the city. Excluding tranquilizers and similar medications, prescriptions are not necessary, so if you have a sample of a regular medicine or can re-

member its name, you can probably obtain the same or similar product manufactured in Mexico (many foreign laboratories are established here). When in doubt, however, always make an appointment with a doctor.

Loss of Passport

If your passport is lost or stolen, contact your embassy:

Canada, Schiller 529, Polanco, tel: 724-79-00
France, Havre 15, Juárez, tel: 533-13-60
Germany: Lord Byron 737, Polanco, tel: 280-54-09
Japan, Reforma 395, Cuauhtémoc, tel: 211-00-28
United Kingdom, Río Lerma 71, Cuauhté-moc, tel: 207-20-89
United States, Reforma 305, Cuauhtémoc, tel: 211-00-42.

For any of the other 60 or so countries with embassies or consulates in Mexico City, check in the Yellow Pages (*Sección Amarilla*), under *embajadas, legaciones y consulado. (*Expect some variation in the spelling of your country's name in Spanish or request the assistance of your hotel staff.)

Ask a policeman

COMMUNICATION AND NEWS
Media

Mexico City has several major dailies in Spanish, including *El Economista, El Financiero, El Sol de México, El Heraldo, Excelsior, UnoMásUno. The News* and *Mexico City Times* are English-language dailies. For what's going on in town, check out *The Mexico City Daily Bulletin*, which is free and available in many hotel lobbies and Sanborns. For an exhaustive weekly listing of entertainment (exhibits, movies, restaurants, shows) get *Tiempo Libre* at newsstands on Thursday (in Spanish). There are also lively magazines, from the glossy *Artes de México* and *Casas y*

No shortage of reading matter

Gente to *fotonovelas* (novels as comics with photos instead of drawings), at corner newsstands or Sanborns (in which you can also find a wide selection of English-language periodicals, as well as a few in German, French and Italian).

Most first-class hotels have cablevision providing US network and cable TV programming, plus local offerings.

Telephone / Fax

The area code for calling into the city from abroad is 5. For direct dialing from Mexico City, consult the *Yellow Pages* for the different codes, but in general 91 and 92 are for calling in Mexico from telephone to telephone and person to person, respectively; 95 and 96 for the US and Canada; and 98 and 99 for other international calls. Fax service (often expensive) is available in the leading hotels and also from public fax machines. Public telephones require a *Cadatel* phonecard available from newsstands and Sanborns.

Mastering the telephone

USEFUL INFORMATION
Tours

For organized tours to the archaeological sites and other places of interest, compare prices and services at the following agencies, which are located on the same street within two blocks of each other. Your hotel will have its own recommendations and may try to persuade you to join their tours.

Expo, Londres 118. Tel: 525-11-49. Offers four-hour tour of downtown Mexico City and Chapultepec Park for $22. Agency's 18 excursions can be by car, minibus or van, depending on the number of people.

Grey Line, Londres 166. Tel: 208-1163. This company offers all-day Mexico City tours including the Cuicuilco pyramid and Xochimilco for about $42, as well as half-day tours and excursions to the pyramids, Mount Popocatépetl and much farther afield (Oaxaca, Guanajuato, and many other locations).

Tratur, through Contur agency, Londres 152. Tel: 525-42-55. Offers a city tour that lasts four hours and costs $30 per person. Buses pick up passengers from their hotels.

If you fancy an inexpensive $5 bus tour of the central area in a charming vehicle that looks like an old trolley, go to the Museo de la Ciudad de México (Mexico City Museum) at Pino Suárez 30, just off the Zócalo, where a tour departs every half hour from 10am–5pm accompanied by a guide.

The cloister at the Franz Mayer Museum

Ecological Tourism

Contact Ecogrupos de México, a young company offering tours to sites where the main attractions are nature and cultural traditions, including a 15-day trip to the Maya world; one week in the Chiapas cloud forest; and one week mostly in Michoacán, stopping over to visit the winter home of the monarch butterflies which fly 2,000 miles from the US to reach this mountain retreat. For further information in the US, call Steppingstone Environmental Education Tours (tel:1-800-874-8784); in Mexico City, tel: 661-9121 or visit their office at Centro Comercial Plaza Inn, Insurgentes Sur 1971.

MUSEUMS

Before planning to visit any of the following (only a partial listing), note that museums in Mexico City are closed on Mondays. Museums usually open at 9 or 10am and close at 5 or 6pm.

Downtown

CUEVAS MUSEUM, Academia 13, tel: 542-89-59. Open Tuesday to Sunday 10am–2pm and 3–6pm. Imaginatively restored former convent housing artist José Luis Cuevas' works.

ALAMEDA MUSEUM (Museo de la Alameda), Cristobal Colón and Balderas. Open Tuesday to Sunday 10am–6pm. Built ex-pressly to house Diego Rivera's great mural *Dream of a Sunday Afternoon in the Alameda,* after the 1985 earthquake, which damaged its previous location, the Hotel del Prado, so severely that it had to be demolished.

BENITO JUAREZ MUSEUM, National Palace, Zócalo, tel: 522-56-46. Open Monday to Friday 10am–6pm. Historical museum honoring the memory of this 19th-century president, sometimes called the Abraham Lincoln of Mexico.

FRANZ MAYER MUSEUM, Hidalgo 45, tel: 518-22-66. Open Tuesday to Sunday 10am–5pm. Marvelous collection of decorative arts furniture, silver and paintings) in one of the most outstanding museums in the city.

MAIN TEMPLE MUSEUM (Museo del Templo Mayor), Guatemala and Seminario, tel. 542-17-17. Open Tuesday to Sunday 9am–5pm. Thousands of pieces discovered during excavations: statues, arrows and knives, jewelry.

MUSEO NACIONAL DE LA CHARRERIA (National Museum of Charro Horsemanship), Isabel la Católica and Izazaga, tel: 521-06-65. Open Monday to Friday 9.30am–7.30pm. Elaborate saddles, spurs, pistols and costumes associated with traditional Mexican horsemanship.

MUSEUM OF THE HISTORY OF MEDICINE (Museo de Historia de la Medicina), Plaza de Santo Domingo, corner of Brasil and Venezuela, tel: 526-12-75. Open Monday to Friday 9am–3pm. History of Mexican medicine from 13th-century Indian remedies up to the present.

MUSEUM OF MEXICO CITY (Museo de la Ciudad de México), Pino Suárez 30, tel: 522-36-40. Open Tuesday to Sunday 10am–6pm. Historic and artistic overview of different eras in the capital's rollercoaster history.

MUSEUM OF THE REVOLUTION (Museo Nacional de la Revolución), Plaza de la República, underneath the Monument to the Revolution free-standing dome, tel: 546-21-15. Open Tuesday to Sunday 9am–5pm. Permanent exhibit on the Mexican Revolution (1910–21).

NATIONAL MUSEUM OF ART (Museo Nacional de Arte), Tacuba 8, tel: 521-733-20. Open Tuesday to Sunday 10am–6pm. Magnificent turn-of-the-century building exhibits Mexican art from the 17th century to 1950.

DOLORES OLMEDO PACIFICO MUSEUM Av Mexico, Coyoacán 5483, La Noria, Xochimilco, tel: 555-0891. Open Tuesday to Sunday 10am–6pm. Beautiful gardens with peacocks surround the museum, which was the residence of Diego Rivera's lover and houses her private collection.

NATIONAL MUSEUM OF CULTURES (Museo Nacional de las Culturas), Moneda 13, tel: 512-74-52. Open Tuesday to Sunday 10am–6pm. Offers an overview of world cultures: prehistoric, Mesopotamian, ancient Egyptian, Greek, Roman, etc. Model rooms.

SAN CARLOS MUSEUM, Puente de Alvarado 50. Open Wednesday to Monday 10am–6pm. European paintings, including works by Goya, Tintoretto, Rubens, Ingres and Mexican masters, and sculpture. Set in former palace designed by Manuel Tolsá.

SOR JUANA INÉS DE LA CRUZ MUSEUM, Plaza de San Jerónimo 47, between Isabel la Católica and 5 de Febrero. Open Tuesday to Friday 9am–2pm. This restored building was once the cloister where Sister Juana Inés, the most famous poetess in Mexican history, lived in the 16th century. It now houses an educational institution offering degree courses in the humanities.

Reforma

MUSEUM OF ANTHROPOLOGY, Paseo de la Reforma and Gandhi. Open Tuesday to Sunday 9am–7pm.

MUSEUM OF HISTORY, Chapultepec Castle, Chapultepec Park. Open Tuesday to Sunday 9am–5pm.

MUSEUM OF MODERN ART (Museo de Arte Moderno), Paseo de la Reforma near Mariano Escobedo. Open Tuesday to Sunday 10am–6pm.

TAMAYO MUSEUM, Paseo de la Reforma and Gandhi. Open Tuesday to Sunday 10am–6pm.

SPORTS

One of the fastest sports alive is the Basque game of **jai alai**, played nightly except Mondays and Wednesdays in the Fronton Mexico (tel: 546-14-69), opposite the Monument to the Revolution. Games have been played continuously here since 1929. Betting is heavy and fun. Games start at 7pm.

The site of two world cup championships, Mexico is a **soccer**-playing country, with the huge Aztec Stadium its largest venue. Enquire at your hotel about the *fútbol* game on Sunday morning. You can get there via the Metro, getting off at the end of the line at Taxqueña and catching the light rail train (*tren ligero*), which will take you right there.

Bullfights are held at the Plaza de Toros Mexico, just off Insurgentes. An afternoon's event usually includes three *toreros* – each 'fighting' and killing two bulls in a highly stylized manner. Two types of seats are available: *sol* (sun), which are cheapest but the least comfortable, and *sombra* (shade).

Horse racing is held at Hipódromo de las Américas. To get there, head through Polanco and up to the end of Ejercito Nacional, from where the entrance is signed. Races are held Saturdays and Sundays, as well as Thursdays most of the year, starting around 2pm.

USEFUL ADDRESSES

Tourist Information

City Tourist Office, Amberes 54, Zona Rosa, tel: 525-93-80. Offers limited information.

Airport Tourist Office, tel: 571-16-63. Staff speak English, French and Spanish.

Airport flight information: 571-32-14

24-hour hotline tourist information service: 250-01-23

INFOTUR Tel: 525-93-80. Offers general information about restaurants, shows, and other entertainment.

FURTHER READING

The range of reading material on Mexico is immense, including history, literature, anthropology, archaeology, art, costumes, arts and crafts.

Painted Walls of Mexico, by Edward Emily and Bravo Alvarez. Documents Mexico's murals, from pre-Columbian times to the post-revolutionary masters – Rivera, Siqueiros, Orozco.

Life in Mexico, by Fanny Calderón de la Barca (Doubleday 1966). One of the best observers ever to visit the country, she was the Scottish wife of the Spanish ambassador to Mexico in the early 19th century.

The Conquest of New Spain, by Bernal Díaz del Castillo (Penguin 1963). The most reliable account of the Conquest, written by one of Cortés's men.

Like Water for Chocolate, by Laura Esquivel (Doubleday 1992). A culinary focus for an unusually successful first novel, on which the applauded movie was based.

Where the Air is Clear, by Carlos Fuentes. The best novel of modern Mexico.

The Lawless Road (published in the US as *Another Mexico*) by Graham Greene. Entertaining account of Greene's travels in Mexico, including his impressions of Catholicism in Mexico.

The Aztecs: Rise and Fall of an Empire, by Serge Gruzinski (New Horizons – Thames and Hudson 1992). One in a series of beautifully designed pocket books, packed with information.

Aztec, by Gary Jennings. Novel describing Aztec life in pre-Cortesian and post-Conquest times.

Mornings in Mexico, by D H Lawrence. Descriptive essays.

Popular Arts of Mexico, by Martìnez Penaloza, one of the outstanding authorities of Mexican art.

The Conquest of Mexico, by William H Prescott. Vivid 19th-century account based on Díaz del Castillo's story.

Distant Neighbors: A Portrait of the Mexicans, by Alan Riding (Harper & Row 1989). Contemporary Mexico as perceived by a foreign journalist.

Sons of the Shaking Earth, by Eric Wolf (University of Chicago Press). Fascinating introduction to Mexico, covering all aspects of life.

Watching the road show

Index

V, W, X, Y, Z

ACKNOWLEDGMENTS

Photography	Marcus Wilson Smith *and*
13, 14, 15B	Antonio García Collection
15T	Museo Nacional de Historia

Production Editor	Mohammed Dar
Handwriting	V Barl
Cover Design	Klaus Geisler
Cartography	Berndtson & Berndtson